Knock, knock.
Who's there?
Lena.
Lena Who?
Lena a little closer and

Knock, knock.
Who's there?
Dishes.
Dishes who?
Dishes your friend, open the door.

Knock, knock.
Who's there?
Daisy.
Daisy who?
Daisy plays, nights he sleeps.

Knock, knock.
Who's there?
Freddie.
Freddie who?
Freddie or not here I come!

"My dog's got no nose."
"Poor thing. How does he smell?"
"Terrible."

Fred: "Are you trying to make as fool out of me?"
Jack: "Oh no, I never interfere with nature."

"Have you got any invisible ink?"
"Certainly, sir. What color?"

What do you do with a sick wasp?
Take it to a waspital.

There was a young man from Quebec
Who wrapped both his legs 'round his kneck
But then he forgot
How to undo the knot
And now he's an absolute wreck!

# 1,000
### Knock Knock Jokes for Kids

# 1,000
### Jokes for Kids of All Ages

# FOR THE
# LAST TIME,
# "WHO'S THERE?"

# 1,000
### Knock Knock Jokes for Kids
# 1,000
### Jokes for Kids of All Ages
# FOR THE LAST TIME, "WHO'S THERE?"

Michael Kilgarriff

BALLANTINE BOOKS · NEW YORK

2007 Ballantine Books Mass Market Edition

*1,000 Jokes for Kids of All Ages* copyright © 1974 by Ward Lock Limited
*1,000 Knock Knock Jokes for Kids* copyright © 1985 by Ward Lock Limited

Published in the United States by Ballantine Books, an imprint of The Random House Publishing Group, a division of Random House, Inc., New York.

BALLANTINE and colophon are registered trademarks of Random House, Inc.

*1,000 Jokes for Kids of All Ages* was originally published in the United States by Ballantine Books, an imprint of The Random House Publishing Group, a division of Random House, Inc., in 1974.

*1,000 Knock Knock Jokes for Kids,* first published in Great Britain in 1985 by Ward Lock Ltd., was originally published in the United States by Ballantine Books, an imprint of The Random House Publishing Group, a division of Random House, Inc., in 1985.

This edition published by arrangement with Ward Lock Ltd.

ISBN 978-0-345-50284-1

Cover design: Jerry Pfeiffer

Printed in the United States of America

www.ballantinebooks.com

OPM 9 8 7 6 5 4 3 2 1

# **Contents**

# 1,000
# Knock Knock Jokes
# for Kids

# Goose Who's Knocking at Your Door

Knock, knock.
*Who's there?*
Goose.
*Goose who?*
Goose who's knocking at your door.

Knock, knock.
*Who's there?*
Bet.
*Bet who?*
Bet you don't know who's knocking on your door!

Knock, knock.
*Who's there?*
Jewel.
*Jewel who?*
Jewel remember me when you see my face.

Knock, knock.
*Who's there?*
Chester.
*Chester who?*
Chester minute! Don't you recognize me?

Knock, knock.
*Who's there?*
Gino.
*Gino who?*
Gino me? Then open the door!

Knock, knock.
*Who's there?*
Alda.
*Alda who?*
Alda time you knew who it was.

Knock, knock.
*Who's there?*
Yacht.
*Yacht who?*
Yacht a know me by now.

Knock, knock.
*Who's there?*
Dishes.
*Dishes who?*
Dishes your friend, open the door.

Will you remember me in one day's time?
*Of course I will.*
Will you remember me in a week's time?
*Of course I will.*
Will you remember me in a year's time?
*Of course I will.*
Will you remember me in ten year's time?
*Of course I will.*
Knock, knock.
*Who's there?*
See—you've forgotten already!

Knock, knock.
*Who's there?*
Ammonia.
*Ammonia who?*
Ammonia gonna tell you once.

Knock, knock.
*Who's there?*
Justin.
*Justin who?*
Justin Quire who is at the door.

3

Knock, knock.
*Who's there?*
Gus.
*Gus who?*
That's what you're supposed to do.

Knock, knock.
*Who's there?*
Wooden Shoe.
*Wooden Shoe who?*
Wooden Shoe like to know!

Knock, knock.
*Who's there?*
Betty.
*Betty who?*
Betty doesn't know who I am.

Knock, knock.
*Who's there?*
Kent.
*Kent who?*
Kent you tell?

Knock, knock.
*Who's there?*
Noah.
*Noah who?*
Noah don't know who either.

Knock, knock.
*Who's there?*
I don't know.
*I don't know who?*
Neither do I, I keep telling you that.

Knock, knock.
*Who's there?*
Howard.
*Howard who?*
Howard I know?

Knock, knock.
*Who's there?*
Emma.
*Emma who?*
Emma glad you asked me that.

Knock, knock.
*Who's there?*
Snow.
*Snow who?*
Snow use, I've lost the little card with my name on it.

Knock, knock.
*Who's there?*
Auto.
*Auto who?*
Auto know, but I've forgotten.

Knock, knock.
*Who's there?*
Jess.
*Jess who?*
Jess me and my shadow.

Knock, knock.
*Who's there?*
One.
*One who?*
One-der why you keep asking that?

Knock, knock.
*Who's there?*
Alma.
*Alma who?*
Alma not going to tell you!

Knock, knock.
*Who's there?*
Zoom.
*Zoom who?*
Zoom do you expect?

Knock, knock.
*Who's there?*
Amy.
*Amy who?*
Amy fraid I've forgotten.

Knock, knock.
*Who's there?*
Arfur.
*Arfur who?*
Arfur got.

Knock, knock.
*Who's there?*
Ewan.
*Ewan who?*
No, just me.

Knock, knock.
*Who's there?*
Cozy.
*Cozy who?*
Cozy who's knocking will you?

Knock, knock.
*Who's ther?*
Sam.
*Sam who?*
Sam person who knocked on the door last time.

Knock, knock.
*Who's there?*
Fozzie.
*Fozzie who?*
Fozzie hundredth time, my name is Nathan!

Knock, knock.
*Who's there?*
Sonia.
*Sonia who?*
Sonia paperboy making a delivery.

Knock, knock.
*Who's there?*
Norma Lee.
*Norma Lee who?*
Norma Lee I don't go around knocking on doors, but you
    see I have this wonderful set of encyclopedias.

Knock, knock.
*Who's there?*
Gerald.
*Gerald who?*
Gerald friend again!

Knock, knock.
*Who's there?*
Specter.
*Specter who?*
Specter Columbo. You're under arrest.

Knock, knock.
*Who's there?*
Diploma.
*Diploma who?*
Diploma to fix the leak.

Knock, knock.
*Who's there?*
Detail.
*Detail who?*
Detail-a-phone operator.

Knock, knock.
*Who's there?*
The Avon Lady. Your bell's broken.

Knock, knock.
*Who's there?*
Doctor.
*Doctor who?*
How did you guess?

Knock, knock.
*Who's there?*
Soup.
*Soup who?*
Soup-erman!

Knock, knock.
*Who's there?*
Ammonia.
*Ammonia who?*
Ammonia little boy who can't reach the doorbell.

Knock, knock.
*Who's there?*
Alka.
*Alka who?*
Alka-pone.

Knock, knock.
*Who's there?*
Cologne.
*Cologne who?*
Cologne Ranger is here!

Knock, knock.
*Who's there?*
Ohio.
*Ohio who?*
Ohio Silver!

Knock, knock.
*Who's there?*
Deduct.
*Deduct who?*
Donald Deduct.

Knock, knock.
*Who's there?*
Sigrid.
*Sigrid who?*
Sigrid service—open up.

Knock, knock.
*Who's there?*
Scissor.
*Scissor who?*
Scissor and Cleopatra.

Knock, knock.
*Who's there?*
N.E.
*N.E. who?*
N.E. body you like so long as you let me in.

Knock, knock.
*Who's there?*
Max.
*Max who?*
Max no difference, just open the door.

Knock, knock.
*Who's there?*
Izzie.
*Izzie who?*
Izzie at the door? You'd better answer it then.

Knock, knock.
*Who's there?*
Amanda.
*Amanda who?*
Amanda fix the television.

# Wotza Name!

Knock, knock.
*Who's there?*
Aaron.
*Aaron who?*
Aaron the barber's floor.

Knock, knock.
*Who's there?*
Abel.
*Abel who?*
Abel seaman.

Knock, knock.
*Who's there?*
Adam.
*Adam who?*
Adam up and tell me the total.

Knock, knock.
*Who's there?*
Adelia.
*Adelia who?*
Adelia the cards after you cut the pack.

Knock, knock.
*Who's there?*
Adeline.
*Adeline who?*
Adeline extra to the letter.

Knock, knock.
*Who's there?*
Alan.
*Alan who?*
Alan't my lesson.

Knock, knock.
*Who's there?*
Aldous.
*Aldous who?*
Aldous who want to leave the room, put your hand up.

Knock, knock.
*Who's there?*
Aldous.
*Aldous who?*
Aldous who aren't interested—go home.

Knock, knock.
*Who's there?*
Alex.
*Alex who?*
Alex Plain later.

Knock, knock.
*Who's there?*
Alfie.
*Alfie who?*
Alfie you in my dreams.

Knock, knock.
*Who's there?*
Alice.
*Alice who?*
Alice N. Tew if you'll listen to me.

Knock, knock.
*Who's there?*
Alma.

*Alma who?*
Alma candy's gone.

Knock, knock.
*Who's there?*
Althea.
*Althea who?*
Althea later this afternoon.

Knock, knock.
*Who's there?*
Amos.
*Amos who?*
Amos-quito bit me.

Knock, knock.
*Who's there?*
Andy.
*Andy who?*
Andy bit me again.

Knock, knock.
*Who's there?*
Anatole.
*Anatole who?*
Anatole me you're a pain in the neck.

Knock, knock.
*Who's there?*
Anderson.
*Anderson who?*
Anderson and daughter came too.

Knock, knock.
*Who's there?*
Andrew.
*Andrew who?*
Andrew a picture of Allison that hurt her feelings.

Knock, knock.
*Who's there?*
Andrew.
*Andrew who?*
Andrew all her money out of the bank.

Knock, knock.
*Who's there?*
Andy.
*Andy who?*
Andy little gadgets to have, door knockers.

Knock, knock.
*Who's there?*
Anita.
*Anita who?*
Anita you like I need a hole in the head.

Knock, knock.
*Who's there?*
Anna.
*Anna who?*
Anna going to tell you anything.

Knock, knock.
*Who's there?*
Anthea.
*Anthea who?*
Anthea get home by 8 o'clock, or else!

Knock, knock.
*Who's there?*
Athena.
*Athena who?*
Athena flying saucer.

Knock, knock.
*Who's there?*
Barry.
*Barry who?*
Barry your bone in the garden, little dog.

Knock, knock.
*Who's there?*
Belinda.
*Belinda who?*
Belinda church steeple.

Knock, knock.
*Who's there?*
Bella.
*Bella who?*
Bella bottom trousers.

Knock, knock.
*Who's there?*
Ben.
*Ben who?*
Ben away a long time.

Knock, knock.
*Who's there?*
Bruce.

*Bruce who?*
I Bruce very easily, don't hit me!

Knock, knock.
*Who's there?*
Buster.
*Buster who?*
Buster the cemetery, please.

Knock, knock.
*Who's there?*
Buster.
*Buster who?*
Buster tire, can I use your phone?

Knock, knock.
*Who's there?*
Carrie.
*Carrie who?*
Carrie me home, I'm tired.

Knock, knock.
*Who's there?*
Celeste.
*Celeste who?*
Celeste time I lend you money.

21

Knock, knock.
*Who's there?*
Chesterfield.
*Chesterfield who?*
Chesterfield full of cows, nothing else.

Knock, knock.
*Who's there?*
Colin.
*Colin who?*
Colin and see me on your way home.

Knock, knock.
*Who's there?*
Colleen.
*Colleen who?*
Colleen up your room, it's filthy.

Knock, knock.
*Who's there?*
Cynthia.
*Cynthia who?*
Cynthia been away so much has happened.

Knock, knock.
*Who's there?*
Cyril.
*Cyril who?*
Cyril pleasure to meet you again.

Knock, knock.
*Who's there?*
Daisy.
*Daisy who?*
Daisy plays, night he sleeps.

Knock, knock.
*Who's there?*
Dana.
*Dana who?*
Dana talk with your mouth full.

Knock, knock.
*Who's there?*
Daryl.
*Daryl who?*
Daryl never be another you!

23

Knock, knock.
*Who's there?*
Dawn.
*Dawn who?*
Dawn leave me standing out here in the cold.

Knock, knock.
*Who's there?*
Deena.
*Deena who?*
Deena hear you the first time.

Knock, knock.
*Who's there?*
Diana.
*Diana who?*
Diana Mals are restless, open the cage.

Knock, knock.
*Who's there?*
Dick.
*Dick who?*
Dick potatoes out of the ground.

Knock, knock.
*Who's there?*

Dinah.
*Dinah who?*
Dinah shoot until you see the whites of their eyes.

Knock, knock.
*Who's there?*
Drucilla.
*Drucilla who?*
Drucilla kid you! You might have got hurt!

Knock, knock.
*Who's there?*
Eddie.
*Eddie who?*
Eddie Body home?

Knock, knock.
*Who's there?*
Edith.
*Edith who?*
Edith'd me on the lipth.

Knock, knock.
*Who's there?*
Eileen.
*Eileen who?*
Eileen over backwards to make you happy.

Knock, knock.
*Who's there?*
Elaine.
*Elaine who?*
Elaine in the country.

Knock, knock.
*Who's there?*
Elsie.
*Elsie who?*
Elsie you around.

Knock, knock.
*Who's there?*
Elsie.
*Elsie who?*
Elsie you later.

Knock, knock.
*Who's there?*
Enoch.
*Enoch who?*
Enoch and Enoch, but nobody opens the door.

Knock, knock.
*Who's there?*

Ernie.
*Ernie who?*
Ernie plenty of money are you?

Knock, knock.
*Who's there?*
Esau.
*Esau who?*
Esau me break the window so let me in quick.

Knock, knock.
*Who's there?*
Esme.
*Esme who?*
Esme petticoat hanging down at the back?

Knock, knock.
*Who's there?*
Esther.
*Esther who?*
Esther anything I can do for you?

Knock, knock.
*Who's there?*
Eugenie.
*Eugenie who?*
Eugenie from the bottle will grant you three wishes.

Knock, knock.
*Who's there?*
Euripedes.
*Euripedes who?*
Euripedes trousers and you'll pay for a new pair!

Knock, knock.
*Who's there?*
Eumenides.
*Eumenides who?*
Eumenides trousers and I won't tell that you ripped them.

Knock, knock.
*Who's there?*
Eva.
*Eva who?*
Eva I told you, would you let me in?

Knock, knock.
*Who's there?*
Evadne.
*Evadne who?*
Evadne problems with your teeth?

Knock, knock.
*Who's there?*
Evadne.

*Evadne who?*
Evadne snails to eat? They're horrible!

Knock, knock.
*Who's there?*
Ezra.
*Ezra who?*
Ezra no hope for me?

Knock, knock.
*Who's there?*
Fanny.
*Fanny who?*
Fanny body calls, I'm out.

Knock, knock.
*Who's there?*
Felix.
*Felix who?*
Felix Ited all over.

Knock, knock.
*Who's there?*
Fiona.
*Fiona who?*
Fiona of the house, I've come for the rent.

Knock, knock.
*Who's there?*
Fiona.
*Fiona who?*
Fiona had something better to do, do you think I'd hang
 around here?

Knock, knock.
*Who's there?*
Fitzwilliam.
*Fitzwilliam who?*
Fitzwilliam better than it fits me.

Knock, knock.
*Who's there?*
Fletcher.
*Fletcher who?*
Fletcher self go.

Knock, knock.
*Who's there?*
Frank.
*Frank who?*
Frankenstein.

Knock, knock.
*Who's there?*

Fred.
*Fred who?*
Fred I can't come out tonight.

Knock, knock.
*Who's there?*
Fred.
*Fred who?*
Fred I'm going to have to leave now.

Knock, knock.
*Who's there?*
Freddie.
*Freddie who?*
Freddie or not, here I come!

Knock, knock.
*Who's there?*
Gay.
*Gay who?*
Gay Topen, that's how the cows got out.

Knock, knock.
*Who's there?*
Gerald.
*Gerald who?*
Gerald washed up.

Knock, knock.
*Who's there?*
Gladys.
*Gladys who?*
Gladys E. Yew.

Knock, knock.
*Who's there?*
Gladys.
*Gladys who?*
Gladys Friday, aren't you?

Knock, knock.
*Who's there?*
Gretel.
*Gretel who?*
Gretel Long little doggie.

Knock, knock.
*Who's there?*
Guthrie.
*Guthrie who?*
Guthrie blind mice.

Knock, knock.
*Who's there?*
Harold.

*Harold who?*
Harold do you think I look?

Knock, knock.
*Who's there?*
Heidi Clare.
*Heidi Clare who?*
Heidi Clare war on you.

Knock, knock.
*Who's there?*
Henrietta.
*Henrietta who?*
Henrietta hat because he lost a bet.

Knock, knock.
*Who's there?*
Howard.
*Howard who?*
Howard you like a punch on the nose?

Knock, knock.
*Who's there?*
Howard.
*Howard who?*
Howard you like to stand out here in the cold while some
    idiot keeps saying "Who's there?"

Knock, knock.
*Who's there?*
Hugh.
*Hugh who?*
Hugh is going to let me in then?

Knock, knock.
*Who's there?*
Hugo.
*Hugo who?*
Hugo first—I'm frightened!

Knock, knock.
*Who's there?*
Ida.
*Ida who?*
Ida know. Sorry!

Knock, knock.
*Who's there?*
Irma.
*Irma who?*
Irma big girl now.

Knock, knock.
*Who's there?*

Isabel.
*Isabel who?*
Isabel on a bike really necessary?

Knock, knock.
*Who's there?*
Ivan.
*Ivan who?*
Ivan my money back.

Knock, knock.
*Who's there?*
Ivan.
*Ivan who?*
Ivan U. Hat, do you like it?

Knock, knock.
*Who's there?*
Jack.
*Jack who?*
Jack Potts.

Knock, knock.
*Who's there?*
Jackson.
*Jackson who?*
Jackson the telephone, you'd better answer it.

Knock, knock.
*Who's there?*
Janet.
*Janet who?*
Janet has too many holes in it, the fish will escape.

Knock, knock.
*Who's there?*
Jeff.
*Jeff who?*
Jeff in one ear, shout!

Knock, knock.
*Who's there?*
Jethro.
*Jethro who?*
Jethro the boat and stop talking so much.

Knock, knock.
*Who's there?*
Jimmy.
*Jimmy who?*
Jimmy a little kiss on the cheek.

Knock, knock.
*Who's there?*

Joan.
*Joan who?*
Joan call us, we'll call you.

Knock, knock.
*Who's there?*
Joe Namath.
*Joe Namath who?*
Joe Namath not on the door, that's why I knocked.

Knock, knock.
*Who's there?*
John.
*John who?*
John me in a cup of tea.

Knock, knock.
*Who's there?*
Josette.
*Josette who?*
Josette down and be quiet.

Knock, knock.
*Who's there?*
Juliet.
*Juliet who?*
Juliet the same amount but she's okay.

Knock, knock.
*Who's there?*
Juno.
*Juno who?*
I dunno, Juno?

Knock, knock.
*Who's there?*
Justin.
*Justin who?*
Justin Casey howls, give him his bottle.

Knock, knock.
*Who's there?*
Justin.
*Justin who?*
Justin time for a cup of tea.

Knock, knock.
*Who's there?*
Justin.
*Justin who?*
Justin time for dinner.

Knock, knock.
*Who's there?*
Kay.

*Kay who?*
Kay, L, M, N, O, P, Q, R, S, T, U, V, W,
   X, Y, Z.

Knock, knock.
*Who's there?*
Kenneth.
*Kenneth who?*
Kenneth little kid play with you?

Knock, knock.
*Who's there?*
Lena.
*Lena who?*
Lena little closer. I want to tell you a secret.

Knock, knock.
*Who's there?*
Liz.
*Liz who?*
Lizen to me when I'm talking to you.

Knock, knock.
*Who's there?*
Liza.
*Liza who?*
Liza wrong to tell.

Knock, knock.
*Who's there?*
Lucretia.
*Lucretia who?*
Lucretia from the Black Lagoon.

Knock, knock.
*Who's there?*
Luke.
*Luke who?*
Luke and see who it is.

Knock, knock.
*Who's there?*
Luke.
*Luke who?*
Luke through the keyhole and see.

Knock, knock.
*Who's there?*
Lydia.
*Lydia who?*
Lydia trash can just blew away.

Knock, knock.
*Who's there?*
Lydia.
*Lydia who?*
Lydia teapot is cracked.

Knock, knock.
*Who's there?*
Lyndon.
*Lyndon who?*
Lyndon ear and I'll tell you.

Knock, knock
*Who's there?*
Mabel.
*Mabel who?*
Mabel doesn't ring either.

Knock, knock
*Who's there?*
Mandy.
*Mandy who?*
Mandy lifeboats, we're sinking.

Knock, knock.
*Who's there?*
Margo.
*Margo who?*
Margo and fetch Pa off the roof, his ladder just broke.

Knock, knock.
*Who's there?*
Matt.
*Matt who?*
Mattadore.

Knock knock.
*Who's there?*
Matthew.
*Matthew who?*
Matthew lace has come undone.

Knock, knock.
*Who's there?*
Max.
*Max who?*
Max no difference—just open the door!

Knock, knock.
*Who's there?*
Michelle.
*Michelle who?*
Michelle had a big crab inside it.

Knock, knock.
*Who's there?*
Mischa.
*Mischa who?*
Mischa a lot.

Knock, knock.
*Who's there?*
Morris.
*Morris who?*
Morris in the pot, help yourself.

Knock, knock.
*Who's there?*
Moses.
*Moses who?*
Moses will you come and have tea with us?

Knock, knock.
*Who's there?*
Nadia.
*Nadia who?*
Nadia head if you understand what I'm saying.

Knock, knock.
*Who's there?*
Nettie.
*Nettie who?*
Nettie as a fruitcake.

Knock, knock.
*Who's there?*
Norman.
*Norman who?*
Norman has ever set foot here before.

Knock, knock.
*Who's there?*
Odysseus.
*Odysseus who?*
Odysseus the final straw!

Knock, knock.
*Who's there?*

Olaf.
*Olaf who?*
Olaf if you think it's that funny!

Knock, knock.
*Who's there?*
Olive.
*Olive who?*
Olive across the road.

Knock, knock.
*Who's there?*
Olive.
*Olive who?*
Olive just around the corner.

Knock, knock.
*Who's there?*
Oliver.
*Oliver who?*
Oliver 'nother one if you've got it.

Knock, knock.
*Who's there?*
Oliver.
*Oliver who?*
Oliver troubles are over.

Knock, knock.
*Who's there?*
Olivia.
*Olivia who?*
Olivia me alone!

Knock, knock.
*Who's there?*
Orson.
*Orson who?*
Orson around again?

Knock, knock.
*Who's there?*
Oscar.
*Oscar who?*
Oscar if she wants a drink.

Knock, knock.
*Who's there?*
Oscar.
*Oscar who?*
Oscar stupid question, you get a stupid answer.

Knock, knock.
*Who's there?*
Patsy.
*Patsy who?*
Patsy dog on the head, he likes it.

Knock, knock.
*Who's there?*
Paul Aidy.
*Paul Aidy who?*
Paul Aidy, she tripped and fell in the mud.

Knock, knock.
*Who's there?*
Paul.
*Paul who?*
Paul hard, the door's stuck again.

Knock, knock.
*Who's there?*
Phil.
*Phil who?*
Phil up my hot water-bottle, I'm cold.

Knock, knock.
*Who's there?*
Philip.
*Philip who?*
Philip the tank, I've got a long way to go.

Knock, knock.
*Who's there?*
Philippa.
*Philippa who?*
Philippa bathtub, I'm dirty.

Knock, knock.
*Who's there?*
Phineas.
*Phineas who?*
Phineas thing happened to me on the way here.

Knock, knock.
*Who's there?*
Phoebe.
*Phoebe who?*
Phoebe too high for us to pay.

Knock, knock.
*Who's there?*
Phyllis.
*Phyllis who?*
Phyllis in on the news.

Knock, knock.
*Who's there?*
Ralph.
*Ralph who?*
Ralph! Ralph! Ralph! I'm your puppy-dog.

Knock, knock.
*Who's there?*
Robin.
*Robin who?*
Robin the pantry is wrong.

Knock, knock.
*Who's there?*
Romeo.
*Romeo who?*
Romeo Ver to the other side of the lake.

Knock, knock.
*Who's there?*
Rosa.
*Rosa who?*
Rosa carrots grow in our garden.

Knock, knock.
*Who's there?*
Roxanne.
*Roxanne who?*
Roxanne pebbles are all over this beach.

Knock, knock.
*Who's there?*
Russell.
*Russell who?*
Russell up something to eat.

Knock, knock.
*Who's there?*
Sacha.
*Sacha who?*
Sacha lot of fuss about nothing.

Knock, knock.
*Who's there?*

Sadie.
*Sadie who?*
Sadie ten times table twice.

Knock, knock.
*Who's there?*
Seth.
*Seth who?*
Seth me, and what I seth goes.

Knock, knock.
*Who's there?*
Seymour.
*Seymour who?*
Seymour if you have a pane of glass in your door.

Knock, knock.
*Who's there?*
Shelly.
*Shelly who?*
Shelly con Carne, a Mexican dish.

Knock, knock.
*Who's there?*
Sonya.
*Sonya who?*
Sonya foot, I can smell it from here.

Knock, knock.
*Who's there?*
Stan.
*Stan who?*
Stan back, I'm coming through.

Knock, knock.
*Who's there?*
Stefan.
*Stefan who?*
Stefan it quick!

Knock, knock.
*Who's there?*
Stella.
*Stella who?*
Stella no answer at the door.

Knock, knock.
*Who's there?*
Tamara.
*Tamara who?*
Tamara the world!

Knock, knock.
*Who's there?*

Thea.
*Thea who?*
Thea later, alligator.

Knock, knock.
*Who's there?*
Theresa.
*Theresa who?*
Theresa fly in my soup.

Knock, knock.
*Who's there?*
Titus.
*Titus who?*
Titus it can be.

Knock, knock.
*Who's there?*
Tobias.
*Tobias who?*
Tobias a pig, that's why I went to market.

Knock, knock.
*Who's there?*
Tyrone.
*Tyrone who?*
Tyrone shoelaces, you're old enough.

Knock, knock.
*Who's there?*
Uriah.
*Uriah who?*
Keep Uriah on the ball.

Knock, knock.
*Who's there?*
Violet.
*Violet who?*
Violet the cat out of the bag?

Knock, knock.
*Who's there?*
Waldo.
*Waldo who?*
Waldo the washing up in the morning.

Knock, knock.
*Who's there?*
Warren.
*Warren who?*
Warren my birthday suit.

Knock, knock.
*Who's there?*
Warren.

*Warren who?*
Warren peace is a famous Russian novel.

Knock, knock.
*Who's there?*
Wayne.
*Wayne who?*
Wayne are you coming over to my house?

Knock, knock.
*Who's there?*
Wendy.
*Wendy who?*
Wendy go? I never saw him.

Knock, knock.
*Who's there?*
William.
*William who?*
William Eynd my bike while I go to the shops?

Knock, knock.
*Who's there?*
William.
*William who?*
William mind your own business!

Knock, knock.
*Who's there?*
Wilma.
*Wilma who?*
Wilma dreams come true?

Knock, knock.
*Who's there?*
Willis.
*Willis who?*
Willis rain never end?

Knock, knock.
*Who's there?*
Willy.
*Willy who?*
Willy make it? I bet he won't!

Knock, knock.
*Who's there?*
Yolande.
*Yolande who?*
Yolande me a dollar, I'll pay you back next week.

Knock, knock.
*Who's there?*
Zena.

*Zena who?*
Zena stealing my books.

Knock, knock.
*Who's there?*
Zenia.
*Zenia who?*
Zenia on TV in that commercial.

# Aries a Reason Why I Talk This Way

Knock, knock.
*Who's there?*
Aries.
*Aries who?*
Aries a reason why I talk this way.

Knock, knock.
*Who's there?*
Adolf.
*Adolf who?*
Adolf ball hit me in the mouth, that's why I talk like this.

Knock, knock.
*Who's there?*
Thayer.
*Thayer who?*
Thayer thorry and I won't throw thisth pie in your fathe.

Knock, knock.
*Who's there?*
Dorrie.
*Dorrie who?*
Dorrie I updet you.

Knock, knock.
*Who's there?*
Canoe.
*Canoe who?*
Canoe come out and play with me?

Knock, nock.
*Who's there?*
Dwayne.
*Dwayne who?*
Dwayne the bathtub. I'm dwowning.

Knock, knock.
*Who's there?*
Sibyl.
*Sibyl who?*
Sibyl Simon met a pieman going to the fair.

Knock, knock.
*Who's there?*
Athol.
*Athol who?*
Athol'd my bike, tho I had to walk.

Knock, knock.
*Who's there?*
Oswald.
*Oswald who?*
Oswald my bubble gum.

Knock, knock
*Who's there?*
Zephyr.
*Zephyr who?*
Zephyr de doctor, I got a code id by node.

Knock, knock.
*Who's there?*
Twain.
*Twain who?*
Twains are what wabbits take a twip on.

Knock, knock.
*Who's there?*

Wayne.
*Wayne who?*
Wayne is coming through the roof.

Knock, knock.
*Who's there?*
Lief.
*Lief who?*
Lief me alone.

Knock, knock.
*Who's there?*
Dishwasher.
*Dishwasher who?*
Dishwasher the way I spoke before I had false teeth.

Knock, knock.
*Who's there?*
Bruce.
*Bruce who?*
I Bruce very easily.

Knock, knock.
*Who's there?*
Toothy.
*Toothy who?*
Toothy ith the day before Wednesday.

Knock, knock.
*Who's there?*
Beth.
*Beth who?*
Beth wisheth, thweetie!

Knock, knock.
*Who's there?*
Althea.
*Althea who?*
Althea later in the afternoon.

Knock, knock.
*Who's there?*
Dishes.
*Dishes who?*
Dishes your friend Margaret, so open the door.

Knock, knock.
*Who's there?*
Dishwasher.
*Dishwasher who?*
Dishwashn't de way I shpoke before I had falsh teeth!

Knock, knock.
*Who's there?*
Wound.

*Wound who?*
Wound and wound the wugged wocks the wagged wascal
  wan.

Knock, knock.
*Who's there?*
Passion.
*Passion who?*
Just Passion by and thought I'd pop in.

Knock, knock.
*Who's there?*
Puss.
*Puss who?*
Puss your bike, it's safer.

Knock, knock.
*Who's there?*
Matthew.
*Matthew who?*
Matthew is pinching my foot.

# Knock Knock
# Dictionary

Knock, knock.
*Who's there?*
Alec.
*Alec who?*
Alec-tricity is shocking.

Knock, knock.
*Who's there?*
Algy.
*Algy who?*
Algy-bra.

Knock, knock.
*Who's there?*
Alma.
*Alma who?*
Alma-nack.

Knock, knock.
*Who's there?*
Amsterdam.
*Amsterdam who?*
Amsterdam is like plum jam, but made from hamsters.

Knock, knock.
*Who's there?*
Anna.
*Anna who?*
Anna-tomical.

Knock, knock.
*Who's there?*
Annie.
*Annie who?*
Annie-versary.

Knock, knock.
*Who's there?*
Ann.
*Ann who?*
Ann-onymous.

Knock, knock.
*Who's there?*
Arthur.
*Arthur who?*
Arthur-itis, it's very painful.

Knock, knock.
*Who's there?*
Arthur.
*Arthur who?*
Arthur-mometer is good for measuring the temperature.

Knock, knock.
*Who's there?*
Bab.
*Bab who?*
Bab Boone is a real ape.

Knock, knock.
*Who's there?*
Bart.
*Bart who?*
Bart-enders serve drinks.

Knock, knock.
*Who's there?*

Bill.
*Bill who?*
Bill-tup area.

Knock, knock.
*Who's there?*
Cameron.
*Cameron who?*
Cameron film are needed to take pictures.

Knock, knock.
*Who's there?*
Cargo.
*Cargo who?*
Cargo "beep beep."

Knock, knock.
*Who's there?*
Clarkeson.
*Clarkeson who?*
Clarkeson watches tell the time.

Knock, knock.
*Who's there?*
Dan.
*Dan who?*
Dan Druff.

Knock, knock.
*Who's there?*
Della.
*Della who?*
Della-katessen.

Knock, knock.
*Who's there?*
Denial.
*Denial who?*
Denial's a river in Egypt.

Knock, knock.
*Who's there?*
Dmitri.
*Dmitri who?*
Dmitri is where lamb chops grow.

Knock, knock.
*Who's there?*
Harris.
*Harris who?*
Harris nice to have on the top of your head.

Knock, knock.
*Who's there?*
Horace.
*Horace who?*
Horace-scopes can be fun.

Knock, knock.
*Who's there?*
Lass.
*Lass who?*
That's what cowboys use, isn't it?

Knock, knock.
*Who's there?*
Maxie.
*Maxie who?*
Maxie-mum.

Knock, knock.
*Who's there?*
Mike.
*Mike who?*
Mike-robe.

Knock, knock.
*Who's there?*
Minnie.
*Minnie who?*
Minnie-mum.

Knock, knock.
*Who's there?*
Miss.
*Miss who?*
Miss L. Toe is nice at Christmas.

Knock, knock.
*Who's there?*
Orson.
*Orson who?*
Orson cart.

Knock, knock.
*Who's there?*
Tennis.
*Tennis who?*
Tennis the sum of five plus five.

Knock, knock.
*Who's there?*

Tilly.
*Tilly who?*
Tilly-vision is my favourite invention.

Knock, knock.
*Who's there?*
Tish.
*Tish who?*
That's good for blowing your nose.

Knock, knock.
*Who's there?*
Tuba.
*Tuba who?*
Tuba toothpaste.

Knock, knock.
*Who's there?*
Walter.
*Walter who?*
Walter wall carpets.

Knock, knock.
*Who's there?*
X.
*X who?*
X can be boiled for breakfast.

Knock, knock.
*Who's there?*
Zombies.
*Zombies who?*
Zombies make honey, others are queens.

# That's a Big Word!

Knock, knock.
*Who's there?*
Allocate.
*Allocate who?*
Allocate, how are you dear?

Knock, knock.
*Who's there?*
Armageddon.
*Armageddon who?*
Armageddon out of here!

Knock, knock.
*Who's there?*
Audacity.
*Audacity who?*
Audacity way to be.

Knock, knock.
*Who's there?*
Bigotry.
*Bigotry who?*
Bigotry than the one in your garden.

Knock, knock.
*Who's there?*
Census.
*Census who?*
Census Saturday we don't have to go to school.

Knock, knock.
*Who's there?*
Denial.
*Denial who?*
Denial's in Egypt, but I'm here.

Knock, knock.
*Who's there?*
Diesel.
*Diesel who?*
Diesel teach you to go around knocking on doors.

Knock, knock.
*Who's there?*
Dynamite.
*Dynamite who?*
Dynamite if you ask her nicely.

Knock, knock.
*Who's there?*
Dinosaur.
*Dinosaur who?*
Dinosaur with you because you called her stupid.

Knock, knock.
*Who's there?*
Disaster.
*Disaster who?*
Disaster be my lucky day.

Knock, knock.
*Who's there?*
Disc.
*Disc who?*
Disc is a recorded message...

Knock, knock.
*Who's there?*

Disease.
*Disease who?*
Disease clothes fit you?

Knock, knock.
*Who's there?*
Disguise.
*Disguise who?*
Disguise the limit!

Knock, knock.
*Who's there?*
Dismay.
*Dismay who?*
Dismay be a joke but it doesn't make me laugh!

Knock, knock.
*Who's there?*
Element.
*Element who?*
Element to tell you that she can't see you today.

Knock, knock.
*Who's there?*
Formosa.
*Formosa who?*
Formosa the summer I was away on my holiday.

Knock, knock.
*Who's there?*
Furlow.
*Furlow who?*
Furlow the leader.

Knock, knock.
*Who's there?*
Grammar.
*Grammar who?*
Grammar is in the Old Peoples' Home.

Knock, knock.
*Who's there?*
Halibut.
*Halibut who?*
Halibut letting me in on the secret?

Knock, knock.
*Who's there?*
Hijack.
*Hijack who?*
Hijack, how's Jill?

Knock, knock.
*Who's there?*
Island.
*Island who?*
Island on your roof with my parachute.

Knock, knock.
*Who's there?*
Ivory.
*Ivory who?*
Ivory strong, like Tarzan.

Knock, knock.
*Who's there?*
Laziness.
*Laziness who?*
Laziness bed all day, when he should be at school.

Knock, knock.
*Who's there?*
Mica.
*Mica who?*
Mica is double-parked, so hurry up!

Knock, knock.
*Who's there?*
Miniature.
*Miniature who?*
Miniature open you mouth you put your foot in it.

Knock, knock.
*Who's there?*
Nuisance.
*Nuisance who?*
What's Nuisance yesterday?

Knock, knock.
*Who's there?*
Ocelot.
*Ocelot who?*
Ocelot of questions, don't you?

Knock, knock.
*Who's there?*
Pharoah.
*Pharoah who?*
Pharoah-nuff.

Knock, knock.
*Who's there?*

Sheik.
*Sheik who?*
Sheik-speare married an Avon lady.

Knock, knock.
*Who's there?*
Sultan.
*Sultan who?*
Sultan Pepper.

Knock, knock.
*Who's there?*
Thermos.
*Thermos who?*
Thermos be a better knock knock joke than this.

Knock, knock.
*Who's there?*
Unite.
*Unite who?*
Unite a person, you call him Sir.

Knock, knock.
*Who's there?*
Virtue.
*Virtue who?*
Virtue get those big brown eyes?

Knock, knock.
*Who's there?*
Wanda.
*Wanda who?*
Wanda buy a cheap bike? It's got no wheels but...

Knock, knock.
*Who's there?*
Zone.
*Zone who?*
Zone shadow scares him.

# Typhoid That Song Before

Knock, knock.
*Who's there?*
Typhoid.
*Typhoid who?*
Typhoid that song before.

Knock, knock.
*Who's there?*
Weasel.
*Weasel who?*
Weasel while you work.

Knock, knock.
*Who's there?*
Wendy.
*Wendy who?*
Wendy red, red robin comes bob, bob, bobbin' along.

Knock, knock.
*Who's there?*
Igloo.
*Igloo who?*
Igloo knew Suzie, like I know Suzie . . .

Knock, knock.
*Who's there?*
Amahl.
*Amahl who?*
Amahl shook up.

Knock, knock.
*Who's there?*
Mia.
*Mia who?*
Mia and my shadow.

Knock, knock.
*Who's there?*
Noah.
*Noah who?*
Noah Body knows the trouble I've seen.

Knock, knock.
*Who's there?*

Rocky.
*Rocky who?*
Rocky bye baby on the tree top.

Knock, knock.
*Who's there?*
Ammonia.
*Ammonia who?*
Ammonia a poor little sparrow...

Knock, knock.
*Who's there?*
Bridget.
*Bridget who?*
London Bridget falling down.

Knock, knock.
*Who's there?*
Ida.
*Ida who?*
Ida know why I love you like I do.

Knock, knock.
*Who's there?*
Caesar.
*Caesar who?*
Caesar jolly good fellow.

Knock, knock.
*Who's there?*
Honda.
*Honda who?*
Honda the spreading chestnut tree.

Knock, knock.
*Who's there?*
Barbara.
*Barbara who?*
Barbara black sheep, have you any wool?

Knock, knock.
*Who's there?*
Sam and Janet.
*Sam and Janet who?*
Sam and Janet evening, you will meet a stranger...

Knock, knock.
*Who's there?*
A Fred.
*A Fred who?*
Who's a Fred of the Big Bad Wolf?

Knock, knock.
*Who's there?*
Heifer.

*Heifer who?*
Heifer dime is better than half a penny...

Knock, knock.
*Who's there?*
Ina Clare.
*Ina Clare who?*
Ina Clare day you can see forever.

Knock, knock.
*Who's there?*
Demon.
*Demon who?*
Demons are a ghoul's best friend.

Knock, knock.
*Who's there?*
Rapunzel.
*Rapunzel who?*
Rapunzel troubles in your old kitbag and smile, smile, smile.

Knock, knock.
*Who's there?*
Aardvark.
*Aardvark who?*
Aardvark a million miles for one of your smiles, my Mammy.

Knock, knock.
*Who's there?*
Kaye.
*Kaye who?*
Kaye sera sera.

Knock, knock.
*Who's there?*
Darren.
*Darren who?*
Darren young man on the flying trapeze.

Knock, knock.
*Who's there?*
Donna.
*Donna who?*
Donna sit under the apple tree with anyone else but me.

Knock, knock.
*Who's there?*
Butcher.
*Butcher who?*
Butcher left leg in, your left leg out...

Knock, knock.
*Who's there?*

Shelby.
*Shelby who?*
Shelby coming 'round the mountain when she comes.

Knock, knock.
*Who's there?*
Sal.
*Sal who?*
Sal-ong way to Tipperary...

Knock, knock.
*Who's there?*
Iguana.
*Iguana who?*
Iguana hold your hand.

Knock, knock.
*Who's there?*
Vaughan.
*Vaughan who?*
Vaughan day my prince vill come.

Knock, knock.
*Who's there?*
Donald.
*Donald who?*
Donald come baby, cradle and all.

Knock, knock.
*Who's there?*
Mayonnaise.
*Mayonnaise who?*
Mayonnaise have seen the glory of the coming of the Lord.

Knock, knock.
*Who's there?*
Hannah.
*Hannah who?*
Hannah partridge in a pear tree.

Knock, knock.
*Who's there?*
Hey.
*Hey who?*
Hey ho, hey ho, it's off to work we go.

Knock, knock.
*Who's there?*
Vera.
*Vera who?*
Vera all the flowers gone.

Knock, knock.
*Who's there?*
Cecil.

*Cecil who?*
Cecil have music wherever she goes.

Knock, knock.
*Who's there?*
Donna Mae.
*Donna Mae who?*
Donna Mae Kew an offer you can't refuse.

Knock, knock.
*Who's there?*
Sonia.
*Sonia who?*
Sonia bird in a gilded cage.

Knock, knock.
*Who's there?*
Weevil.
*Weevil who?*
Weevil work it out.

# Midas Well Open the Door 'cause I'm Not Going Away!

Knock, knock.
*Who's there?*
Midas.
*Midas who?*
Midas well open the door 'cause I'm not going away.

Knock, knock.
*Who's there?*
Jennie.
*Jennie who?*
Jennie-d any help opening the door?

Knock, knock.
*Who's there?*
Ivan.
*Ivan who?*
Ivan idea you don't want to see me.

Knock, knock.
*Who's there?*
Fanny.
*Fanny who?*
Fanny body gonna open this door then?

Knock, knock.
*Who's there?*
Eileen.
*Eileen who?*
Eileen Don your bell and broke it.

Knock, knock.
*Who's there?*
Fanny.
*Fanny who?*
Fanny the way you keep saying "Who's there?" every time
   I knock!

Knock, knock.
*Who's there?*
Howard.
*Howard who?*
Howard you know unless you open the door?

Knock, knock.
*Who's there?*
Anna.
*Anna who?*
Anna Nother thing, how many times do I have to knock
on this door before you open up?

Knock, knock.
*Who's there?*
Dishes.
*Dishes who?*
Dishes getting boring!

Knock, knock.
*Who's there?*
Lettuce.
*Lettuce who?*
Lettuce in, won't you?

Knock, knock.
*Who's there?*
Ivor.
*Ivor who?*
Ivor sore hand from knocking on your door!

Knock, knock.
*Who's there?*
Luke.
*Luke who?*
Luke through the keyhole and you'll see.

Knock, knock.
*Who's there?*
Isabel.
*Isabel who?*
Isabel broken, 'cause I had to knock?!

Knock, knock.
*Who's there?*
Mavis.
*Mavis who?*
Mavis be the last time I knock on this door.

Knock, Knock.
*Who's there?*
Thistle.
*Thistle who?*
Thistle be the last time I knock on this door.

Knock, knock.
*Who's there?*
Eggs.
*Eggs who?*
Eggstremely cold waiting for you to open the door.

Knock, knock.
*Who's there?*
Waddle.
*Waddle who?*
Waddle you give me to go away?

Knock, knock.
*Who's there?*
Heywood, Hugh, Harry.
*Heywood, Hugh, Harry who?*
Heywood Hugh Harry up and open this door.

Knock, knock.
*Who's there?*
Dozen.
*Dozen who?*
Dozen anyone live here anymore?

Knock, knock.
*Who's there?*

Des.
*Des who?*
Des no bell, dat's why I'm knocking.

Knock, knock.
*Who's there?*
Hobbit.
*Hobbit who?*
Hobbit letting me in then?

Knock, knock.
*Who's there?*
Darwin.
*Darwin who?*
I'll be Darwin you open the door.

Knock, knock.
*Who's there?*
Havelock.
*Havelock who?*
Havelock put on your door.

Knock, knock.
*Who's there?*
Tillie.
*Tillie who?*
Tillie comes I'm going to wait here.

Knock, knock.
*Who's there?*
Olga.
*Olga who?*
Olga home if you don't open up.

Knock, knock.
*Who's there?*
Juan.
*Juan who?*
Juan of these days you'll find out!

Knock, knock.
*Who's there?*
Earl.
*Earl who?*
Earl be glad to tell you if you open the door.

Knock, knock.
*Who's there?*
Eliza.
*Eliza who?*
Eliza wake at night thinking about this door.

Knock, knock.
*Who's there?*
Isabella.
*Isabella who?*
Isabella dropped off so you not hear?

Knock, knock.
*Who's there?*
Abbot.
*Abbot who?*
Abbot time you opened this door!

Knock, knock.
*Who's there?*
Xavier.
*Xavier who?*
Xavier breath, I'm not leaving.

Knock, knock.
*Who's there?*
Ferdie.
*Ferdie who?*
Ferdie last time, open the door!

Knock, knock.
*Who's there?*
Avon.
*Avon who?*
Avon to get in.

Tap, tap.
*Who's there?*
Hurd.
*Hurd who?*
Hurd my hand, so I couldn't knock-knock.

Knock, knock.
*Who's there?*
Harry.
*Harry who?*
Harry up and let me in!

Knock, knock.
*Who's there?*
Don.
*Don who?*
Don mess about, just open the door.

Knock, knock.
*Who's there?*

Doris.
*Doris who?*
Doris dropping off its hinges with all this knocking.

Knock, knock.
*Who's there?*
Savannah.
*Savannah who?*
Savannah you going to open the door?

Knock, knock.
*Who's there?*
Sis.
*Sis who?*
Sis any way to treat a friend?

Knock, knock.
*Who's there?*
Ammonia.
*Ammonia who?*
Ammonia gonna tell you once.

Knock, knock.
*Who's there?*
Isadore.
*Isadore who?*
Isadore open or locked?

Knock, knock.
*Who's there?*
Theodore.
*Theodore who?*
Theodore wasn't open so I knocked-knocked.

Knock, knock.
*Who's there?*
Ken.
*Ken who?*
Ken I come in?

Knock, knock.
*Who's there?*
Justice.
*Justice who?*
Justice I thought—no one at home.

Knock, knock; ting-a-ling.
*Who's there?*
UCI.
*UCI who?*
UCI had to ring because you didn't answer when I knocked.

Knock, knock.
*Who's there?*
Sincerely.

*Sincerely who?*
Sincerely this morning I've been waiting for you to open
    this door.

Knock, knock.
*Who's there?*
Lucinda.
*Lucinda who?*
Lucinda chain, I want to get in.

Knock, knock.
*Who's there?*
Adore.
*Adore who?*
Adore stands between us, open up!

Knock, knock.
*Who's there?*
Usher.
*Usher who?*
Usher wish you would let me in.

Knock, knock.
*Who's there?*
Martini.
*Martini who?*
Martini hand is frozen so let me in!

Knock, knock.
*Who's there?*
Betty.
*Betty who?*
Betty things to do than stand here, you know.

Knock, knock.
*Who's there?*
Freighter.
*Freighter who?*
Frieghter open the door?

Knock, knock.
*Who's there?*
Stan.
*Stan who?*
Stan back, I'm knocking the door down.

Knock, knock.
*Who's there?*
Dozen.
*Dozen who?*
Dozen anyone want to let me in?

Knock, knock.
*Who's there?*

Stepfather.
*Stepfather who?*
One stepfather and I'll be in.

Knock, knock.
*Who's there?*
You.
*You who?*
You who! Is there anybody in?

Knock, knock.
*Who's there?*
Ken.
*Ken who?*
Ken you open the door and let me in?

Knock, knock.
*Who's there?*
Owen.
*Owen who?*
Owen are you going to let me in?

Knock, knock.
*Who's there?*
Emmett.
*Emmett who?*
Emmett the back door, not the front.

Knock, knock.
*Who's there?*
Olga.
*Olga who?*
Olga way when I'm good and ready.

Knock, knock.
*Who's there?*
Sarah.
*Sarah who?*
Sarah 'nother way into this building?

Knock, knock.
*Who's there?*
Ice cream.
*Ice cream who?*
Ice cream if you don't let me in.

Knock, knock.
*Who's there?*
Howell.
*Howell who?*
Howell I get in if you don't open the door.

Knock, knock.
*Who's there?*
Lettuce.

*Lettuce who?*
Lettuce in, won't you?

Knock, knock.
*Who's there?*
Ali.
*Ali who?*
Ali-luyah, at last you've opened the door.

# Norma Lee I Wouldn't Have Troubled You, But...

Knock, knock.
*Who's there?*
Norma Lee.
*Norma Lee who?*
Norma Lee I wouldn't have troubled you, but I need help.

Knock, knock.
*Who's there?*
Mister.
*Mister who?*
Mister last bus home.

Knock, knock.
*Who's there?*
Anne.
*Anne who?*
Anne apple just fell on my head.

Knock, knock.
*Who's there?*
Mickey.
*Mickey who?*
Mickey's stuck in the lock!

Knock, knock.
*Who's there?*
Police.
*Police who?*
Police open the door. I have to go to the bathroom.

Knock, knock.
*Who's there?*
Madam.
*Madam who?*
Madam finger's caught in the door.

Knock, knock.
*Who's there?*
Musket.
*Musket who?*
Musket in, it's urgent.

Knock, knock.
*Who's there?*
Butter.
*Butter who?*
Butter be quick, I have to go to the bathroom.

Knock, knock.
*Who's there?*
Mickey.
*Mickey who?*
Mickey dropped down the drain.

Knock, knock.
*Who's there?*
Doris.
*Doris who?*
Doris jammed again.

Knock, knock.
*Who's there?*
Yelp.
*Yelp who?*
Yelp me! My nose is stuck in the keyhole.

Knock, knock.
*Who's there?*
Scold.

*Scold who?*
Scold outside.

Knock, knock.
*Who's there?*
Gutter.
*Gutter who?*
Gutter get in, it's snowing out here.

Knock, knock.
*Who's there?*
Ken.
*Ken who?*
Ken I Cummin, it's freezing out here?

Knock, knock.
*Who's there?*
Diana.
*Diana who?*
Diana thirst, can I have some water please?

Knock, knock.
*Who's there?*
Doris.
*Doris who?*
Doris slammed on my finger so open it quick.

# Lauren Order

Knock, knock.
*Who's there?*
Lauren.
*Lauren who?*
Lauren order.

Knock, knock.
*Who's there?*
Dwight.
*Dwight who?*
Dwight way and a wrong way.

Knock, knock.
*Who's there?*
Faye.
*Faye who?*
Faye Kearings.

Knock, knock.
*Who's there?*
Wanda.
*Wanda who?*
Wanda around while I climb through the window.

Knock, knock.
*Who's there?*
Ammon.
*Ammon who?*
Ammon old hand at picking locks.

Knock, knock.
*Who's there?*
Robin.
*Robin who?*
Robin the piggy bank again.

Knock, knock.
*Who's there?*
Barry.
*Barry who?*
Barry the treasure where no one will find it.

Knock, knock.
*Who's there?*
Razor.
*Razor who?*
Razor hands—this is a stick-up!

Knock, knock.
*Who's there?*
Andrew.
*Andrew who?*
Andrew all over the wall, and boy is she in big trouble.

Knock, knock.
*Who's there?*
Stopwatch.
*Stopwatch who?*
Stopwatch you're doing this instant!

Knock, knock.
*Who's there?*
Colleen.
*Colleen who?*
Colleen all cars!

Knock, knock.
*Who's there?*

Dishes.
*Dishes who?*
Dishes the police, open up!

Knock, knock.
*Who's there?*
Iris.
*Iris who?*
Iris Tew in the name of the law.

Knock, knock.
*Who's there?*
Quiet Tina.
*Quiet Tina who?*
Quiet Tina court room please.

Knock, knock.
*Who's there?*
Lionel.
*Lionel who?*
Lionel get you nowhere, better tell the truth.

Knock, knock.
*Who's there?*
Delores.
*Delores who?*
Delores on the side of good people.

Knock, knock.
*Who's there?*
Geordie.
*Geordie who?*
Geordie-rectly to jail, do not pass go, do not collect $200 . . .

Knock, knock.
*Who's there?*
Kermit.
*Kermit who?*
Kermit a crime and you'll get locked up.

Knock, knock.
*Who's there?*
Lady.
*Lady who?*
Lady law down.

Knock, knock.
*Who's there?*
Sinbad.
*Sinbad who?*
Sinbad and you'll never to go Heaven.

Knock, knock.
*Who's there?*
Toyota.
*Toyota who?*
Toyota be a law against knock knock jokes.

# Bonanza!

Knock, knock.
*Who's there?*
Lettuce.
*Lettuce who?*
Lettuce tell you a few good knock knock jokes.

Knock, knock.
*Who's there?*
Izzy.
*Izzy who?*
Izzy come, izzy go.

Knock, knock.
*Who's there?*
Omar.
*Omar who?*
Omar goodness gracious! Wrong door!

Knock, knock.
*Who's there?*
Odette.
*Odette who?*
Odette's a bad sign.

Knock, knock.
*Who's there?*
Les.
*Les who?*
Les go out for a picnic.

Knock, knock.
*Who's there?*
Knock, knock.
*Who's there?*
Knock, knock.
*Who's there?*
Knock, knock.
*Who's there?*
I'm sorry, but my mother doesn't allow me to speak to
    strangers.

Knock, knock.
*Who's there?*
Says.
*Says who?*
Says me, that's who!

Knock, knock.
*Who's there?*
An author.
*An author who?*
An author joke like this and I'm off!

Knock, knock.
*Who's there?*
Pill.
*Pill who?*
Yes please, and a sheet to go with it.

Knock, knock.
*Who's there?*
Doughnut.
*Doughnut who?*
Doughnut open your presents until Christmas Day.

Knock, knock.
*Who's there?*
Donalette.
*Donalette who?*
Donalette the bed bugs bite.

Knock, knock.
*Who's there?*

Abba.
*Abba who?*
Abba banana.

Knock, knock.
*Who's there?*
Duck.
*Duck who?*
Just duck! They're throwing things at us.

Knock, knock.
*Who's there?*
Gorilla.
*Gorilla who?*
Gorilla cheese sandwich for me and I'll be right over.

Knock, knock.
*Who's there?*
Cassette.
*Cassette who?*
Cassette your dinner, I'm sorry.

Knock, knock.
*Who's there?*
Hammond.
*Hammond who?*
Hammond cheese on toast, please.

Knock, knock.
*Who's there?*
Amanda.
*Amanda who?*
Amanda-rin orange.

Knock, knock.
*Who's there?*
Fido.
*Fido who?*
Fido I have to wait here?

Knock, knock.
*Who's there?*
Bernadette.
*Bernadette who?*
Bernadette all my dinner.

Knock, knock.
*Who's there?*
Tank.
*Tank who?*
You're welcome.

Knock, knock.
*Who's there?*

House.
*House who?*
Oh, Hugh's fine thank you.

Knock, knock.
*Who's there?*
Pencil.
*Pencil who?*
Your Pencil fall down if the elastic goes.

Knock, knock.
*Who's there?*
Eyes.
*Eyes who?*
Eyes got loads more knock knock jokes for you.

Knock, knock.
*Who's there?*
P.
*P. who?*
P. Nuts are an elephant's favorite treat.

Knock, knock.
*Who's there?*
Who.
*Who who?*
Bad echo in here, isn't there!

Knock, knock.
*Who's there?*
Pizza.
*Pizza who?*
Pizza cake would be great right now.

Knock, knock.
*Who's there?*
Closure.
*Closure who?*
Closure mouth when you eat.

Knock, knock.
*Who's there?*
General Lee.
*General Lee who?*
General Lee I don't mind school dinners.

Knock, knock.
*Who's there?*
Alec.
*Alec who?*
Alec coffee, but I don't like tea.

Knock, knock.
*Who's there?*
Harriet.
*Harriet who?*
Harriet all my lunch, I'm starving.

Knock, knock.
*Who's there?*
Gorilla.
*Gorilla who?*
Gorilla me a hamburger.

Knock, knock.
*Who's there?*
Wooden.
*Wooden who?*
Wooden you like to know.

Knock, knock.
*Who's there?*
Punch.
*Punch who?*
Not me, please!

Knock, knock.
*Who's there?*
Boo.
*Boo who?*
Just boo! I'm a ghost.

Ring! Ring!
*Who's there?*
Hurd my.
*Hurd my who?*
Hurd my hand so I can't knock.

Knock, knock.
*Who's there?*
One-eye.
*One-eye who?*
You're the One-eye care for.

Knock, knock.
*Who's there?*
Jupiter.
*Jupiter who?*
Jupiter hurry, or you'll miss the bus.

Knock, knock.
*Who's there?*

Bean.
*Bean who?*
Bean working very hard today.

Knock, knock.
*Who's there?*
Heaven.
*Heaven who?*
Heaven seen you for a long time.

Knock, knock.
*Who's there?*
Hope.
*Hope who?*
Hopefully that present is for me.

Knock, knock.
*Who's there?*
Bertha.
*Bertha who?*
Bertha-day greetings.

Knock, knock.
*Who's there?*
Dragon.
*Dragon who?*
Dragon your feet again.

Knock, knock.
*Who's there?*
Adlai.
*Adlai who?*
Adlai a bet on that.

Knock, knock.
*Who's there?*
Cows.
*Cows who?*
Cows go "moo" not "who"!

Knock, knock.
*Who's there?*
Tuna fish.
*Tuna fish who?*
You can tune a piano, but you can't tuna fish.

Knock, knock.
*Who's there?*
Consumption.
*Consumption who?*
Consumption be done about all these knock knock jokes?

Knock, knock.
*Who's there?*
Argo.
*Argo who?*
Argo to the beach for my holidays.

Knock, knock.
*Who's there?*
Stanton.
*Stanton who?*
Stanton here in the cold is no fun.

Knock, knock.
*Who's there?*
Jaws.
*Jaws who?*
Jaws truly.

Knock, knock.
*Who's there?*
Tuna.
*Tuna who?*
Tuna your radio down, I'm trying to get some sleep.

Knock, knock.
*Who's there?*
Lettuce.
*Lettuce who?*
Lettuce try again tomorrow.

Knock, knock.
*Who's there?*
X.
*X who?*
X-tremely pleased to meet you.

Knock, knock.
*Who's there?*
Major.
*Major who?*
Major B. Hindsor when you got spanked.

Knock, knock.
*Who's there?*
Banana.
*Banana who?*
Banana split so ice creamed.

Knock, knock.
*Who's there?*

Annetta.
*Annetta who?*
Annetta joke like that and you're off this bus.

Knock, knock.
*Who's there?*
Haydn.
*Haydn who?*
Haydn seek is fun to play.

Knock, knock.
*Who's there?*
Farmer.
*Farmer who?*
Farmer birthday I'm going to have a new bike.

Knock, knock.
*Who's there?*
Osborne.
*Osborne who?*
Osborne today, it's my birthday.

Knock, knock.
*Who's there?*
Lock.
*Lock who?*
Lock who it is, after all this time!

Knock, knock.
*Who's there?*
Turnip.
*Turnip who?*
Turnip for work at nine or you're fired!

Knock, knock.
*Who's there?*
Nana.
*Nana who?*
Nana your business.

Knock, knock.
*Who's there?*
Rhoda.
*Rhoda who?*
Rhoda boat as fast as you can.

Knock, knock.
*Who's there?*
Amory.
*Amory who?*
Amory Christmas and a happy New Year to all our
    readers.

Knock, knock.
*Who's there?*
Athena.
*Athena who?*
Athena reindeer landing on your roof.

Knock, knock.
*Who's there?*
Gilda.
*Gilda who?*
Gilda fly that sat on the end of my nose.

Knock, knock.
*Who's there?*
Quacker.
*Quacker who?*
Quacker 'nother bad joke and I'm off!

Knock, knock.
*Who's there?*
Datsun.
*Datsun who?*
Datsun old joke.

Knock, knock.
*Who's there?*
Deceit.
*Deceit who?*
Deceit of your trousers looks wet.

Knock, knock.
*Who's there?*
Noah.
*Noah who?*
Noah yes—which is it?

Knock, knock.
*Who's there?*
Ollie.
*Ollie Who?*
Ollie time you do that I want to scream!

Knock, knock.
*Who's there?*
Hominy.
*Hominy who?*
Hominy people live in this house?

Knock, knock.
*Who's there?*

Ivan.
*Ivan who?*
Ivan idea you know who it is.

Knock, knock.
*Who's there?*
Watson.
*Watson who?*
Watson the menu today?

Knock, knock.
*Who's there?*
Europe.
*Europe who?*
Europe early this morning.

Knock, knock.
*Who's there?*
Meg.
*Meg who?*
Meg your bed before you get any breakfast.

Knock, knock.
*Who's there?*
Aida.
*Aida who?*
Aida huge breakfast before going to school.

Knock, knock.
*Who's there?*
Howell.
*Howell who?*
Howell you have your toast, with marmalade or jam?

Knock, knock.
*Who's there?*
Egbert.
*Egbert who?*
Egbert no bacon.

Knock, knock.
*Who's there?*
Boiler.
*Boiler who?*
Boiler egg for four minutes.

Knock, knock.
*Who's there?*
Hammond.
*Hammond who?*
Hammond eggs.

Knock, knock.
*Who's there?*

Farmer.
*Farmer who?*
Farmer people here than there were last year.

Knock, knock.
*Who's there?*
Turnip.
*Turnip who?*
Turnip the heat, it's cold in here.

Knock, knock.
*Who's there?*
Man.
*Man who?*
Managed to get here then.

Knock, knock.
*Who's there?*
Kipper.
*Kipper who?*
Kipper hands to yourself.

Knock, knock.
*Who's there?*
York.
*York who?*
York coming over to our place.

Knock, knock.
*Who's there?*
Alison.
*Alison who?*
Alison to my radio in the mornings.

Knock, knock.
*Who's there?*
Doughnut.
*Doughnut who?*
Doughnut let anyone else in but me.

Knock, knock.
*Who's there?*
Fodder.
*Fodder who?*
Fodder and mother are taking me on holiday.

Knock, knock.
*Who's there?*
Darius.
*Darius who?*
Darius a lot I have to tell you.

Knock, knock.
*Who's there?*

Odessa.
*Odessa who?*
Odessa really funny face, man!

Knock, knock.
*Who's there?*
Zookeeper.
*Zookeeper who?*
Zookeeper way from me!

Knock, knock.
*Who's there?*
Cindy.
*Cindy who?*
Cindy next one in please.

Knock, knock.
*Who's there?*
Ether.
*Ether who?*
Ether bunny.

Knock, knock.
*Who's there?*
Plato.
*Plato who?*
Plato fish and chips please.

Knock, knock.
*Who's there?*
Dinah.
*Dinah who?*
Dinah is served.

Knock, knock.
*Who's there?*
Emma.
*Emma who?*
Emma pig when it comes to ice cream.

Knock, knock.
*Who's there?*
Roland.
*Roland who?*
Roland butter please.

Knock, knock.
*Who's there?*
Maida.
*Maida who?*
Maida cake 'cause you were coming.

Knock, knock.
*Who's there?*
Carmen.
*Carmen who?*
Carmen get it!

Knock, knock.
*Who's there?*
Genoa.
*Genoa who?*
Genoa new knock knock joke?

Knock, knock.
*Who's there?*
Nose.
*Nose who?*
I nose plenty more knock knock jokes, don't worry!

# Moira See You, Moira Like You!

Knock, knock.
*Who's there?*
Moira.
*Moira who?*
Moira see you, Moira like you!

Knock, knock.
*Who's there?*
Cynthia.
*Cynthia who?*
Cynthia been gone I mith you very much.

Knock, knock.
*Who's there?*
Alfalfa.
*Alfalfa who?*
Alfalfa you if you fall for me.

Knock, knock.
*Who's there?*
Hollis.
*Hollis who?*
Hollis forgiven, come home.

Knock, knock.
*Who's there?*
Wah.
*Wah who?*
Well, you don't have to get excited just because I'm here!

Knock, knock.
*Who's there?*
Wicked.
*Wicked who?*
Wicked go for long walks together.

Knock, knock.
*Who's there?*
Eyesore.
*Eyesore who?*
Eyesore do like you.

Knock, knock.
*Who's there?*
Value.
*Value who?*
Value be my Valentine?

Knock, knock.
*Who's there?*
Butcher.
*Butcher who?*
Butcher arms around me.

Knock, knock.
*Who's there?*
Honeydew.
*Honeydew who?*
Honeydew you want to come out tonight?

Knock, knock.
*Who's there?*
Olive.
*Olive who?*
Olive you too, Honeybunch!

Knock, knock.
*Who's there?*

Guinevere.
*Guinevere who?*
Guinevere going to get together again?

Knock, knock.
*Who's there?*
Sauce.
*Sauce who?*
Sauce together, now she'll tell everyone.

Knock, knock.
*Who's there?*
Felix.
*Felix who?*
Felix Ited, about meeting you.

Knock, knock.
*Who's there?*
Anthem.
*Anthem who?*
U. Anthem devil you.

Knock, knock.
*Who's there?*
Alice.
*Alice who?*
Alice forgiven, please come home.

Knock, knock.
*Who's there?*
Pyjamas.
*Pyjamas who?*
Pyjamas 'round me honey, hold me tight.

Knock, knock.
*Who's there?*
Gwen.
*Gwen who?*
Gwen will I see you again?

Knock, knock.
*Who's there?*
Sherry.
*Sherry who?*
Sherry dance?

Knock, knock.
*Who's there?*
Murray.
*Murray who?*
Murray me! Not likely!

Knock, knock.
*Who's there?*
Oliver.

*Oliver who?*
Oliver, but she doesn't love me.

Knock, knock.
*Who's there?*
Congo.
*Congo who?*
Congo on meeting like this.

Knock, knock.
*Who's there?*
Myth.
*Myth who?*
Myth you too.

# Yukon Say That Again

## *Buddha This Slice of Bread for Me*
### or
## *Wise Sayings from the East*

Knock, knock.
*Who's there?*
Buddha.
*Buddha who?*
Buddha this slice of bread for me.

Knock, knock.
*Who's there?*
Yulla.
*Yulla who?*
Yulla catch more flies with honey than vinegar.

Knock, knock.
*Who's there?*
Zeke.
*Zeke who?*
Zeke and ye shall find.

Knock, knock.
*Who's there?*
Pudding.
*Pudding who?*
Pudding on your shoes before your trousers is a bad idea.

Knock, knock.
*Who's there?*
Tish.
*Tish who?*
Tish who is good for blowing your nose.

Knock, knock.
*Who's there?*
Carlotta.
*Carlotta who?*
Carlotta trouble when it breaks down.

Knock, knock.
*Who's there?*
Cargo.
*Cargo who?*
Cargo better if you fill it with gas first.

Knock, knock.
*Who's there?*
Your pencil.
*Your pencil who?*
Your pencil fall down if you don't wear a belt or suspenders.

Knock, knock.
*Who's there?*
Fiddlestick.
*Fiddlestick who?*
Fiddlestick out of the bottom of the bed if you're too tall.

Knock, knock.
*Who's there?*
Seymour.
*Seymour who?*
Seymour if you look out of the window.

Knock, knock.
*Who's there?*
Lionel.
*Lionel who?*
Lionel roar if you don't feed him.

Knock, knock.
*Who's there?*
Lucy.
*Lucy who?*
Lucy Lastic can be embarrassing.

Knock, knock.
*Who's there?*
Luke.
*Luke who?*
Luke before you leap.

Knock, knock.
*Who's there?*
Constance Norah.
*Constance Norah who?*
Constance Norahs makes it difficult to sleep.

Knock, knock.
*Who's there?*
Howard.
*Howard who?*
Howard the ground is when you slip on a banana skin.

Knock, knock.
*Who's there?*
Wanda.
*Wanda who?*
Wanda off and you'll get lost.

Knock, knock.
*Who's there?*
Cattle.
*Cattle who?*
Cattle always purr when you stroke her.

Knock, knock.
*Who's there?*
Lucifer.
*Lucifer who?*
Lucifer coat and you'll be cold.

Knock, knock.
*Who's there?*

Tuna.
*Tuna who?*
Tuna violin and it will sound better.

## *Familiar Phrases*

Knock, knock.
*Who's there?*
Yukon.
*Yukon who?*
Yukon say that again.

Knock, knock.
*Who's there?*
Ellie.
*Ellie who?*
Ellie Phants never forget.

Knock, knock.
*Who's there?*
Denver.
*Denver who?*
Denver the good old days.

Knock, knock.
*Who's there?*
Percy.
*Percy who?*
Percy Vere and you'll succeed.

Knock, knock.
*Who's there?*
Spook.
*Spook who?*
Spook only when you are spoken to.

Knock, knock.
*Who's there?*
Wannetta.
*Wannetta who?*
Wannetta time, please!

Knock, knock.
*Who's there?*
Schatzi.
*Schatzi who?*
Schatzi way to do it.

Knock, knock.
*Who's there?*

John.
*John who?*
John the Navy and see the world.

Knock, knock.
*Who's there?*
Sizzle.
*Sizzle who?*
Sizzle hurt me more than it will you.

Knock, knock.
*Who's there?*
Omega.
*Omega who?*
Omega best man win.

Knock, knock.
*Who's there?*
Teddy.
*Teddy who?*
Teddy is the beginning of the rest of your life.

Knock, knock.
*Who's there?*
Emile.
*Emile who?*
Emile fit for a king.

Knock, knock.
*Who's there?*
Toucan.
*Toucan who?*
Toucan live as cheaply as one.

Knock, knock.
*Who's there?*
Yukon.
*Yukon who?*
Yukon fool some of the people some of the time...

Knock, knock.
*Who's there?*
Tex.
*Tex who?*
Tex two to tango.

Knock, knock.
*Who's there?*
Willoughby.
*Willoughby who?*
Willoughby a monkey's uncle!

Knock, knock.
*Who's there?*

Arnold.
*Arnold who?*
Arnold friend of yours is a friend of mine.

Knock, knock.
*Who's there?*
Zizi.
*Zizi who?*
Zizi when you know how.

Knock, knock.
*Who's there?*
Dawn.
*Dawn who?*
Dawn do anything I wouldn't do.

Knock, knock.
*Who's there?*
Hair.
*Hair who?*
Hair today and gone tomorrow.

Knock, knock.
*Who's there?*
Sharon.
*Sharon who?*
Sharon share alike.

Knock, knock.
*Who's there?*
Cigarette.
*Cigarette who?*
Cigarette life if you don't weaken.

Knock, knock.
*Who's there?*
Mortimer.
*Mortimer who?*
Mortimer than meets the eye.

Knock, knock.
*Who's there?*
Lilac.
*Lilac who?*
Lilac a trooper.

Knock, knock.
*Who's there?*
Watusi.
*Watusi who?*
Watusi is what you get.

Knock, knock.
*Who's there?*
Eustace.
*Eustace who?*
Come Eustace you are.

Knock, knock.
*Who's there?*
Sofa.
*Sofa who?*
Sofa so good.

Knock, knock.
*Who's there?*
Radio.
*Radio who?*
Radio not, here I come.

Knock, knock.
*Who's there?*
Don.
*Don who?*
Don just stand there, say something.

# Clichés

Knock, knock.
*Who's there?*
Holmes.
*Holmes who?*
Holmes is where the heart is.

Knock, knock.
*Who's there?*
Roland.
*Roland who?*
Roland stone gathers no moss.

Knock, knock.
*Who's there?*
Manny.
*Manny who?*
Manny are called, but few are chosen.

Knock, knock.
*Who's there?*
Burton.
*Burton who?*
Burton the hand is worth two in the bush.

Knock, knock.
*Who's there?*
Dotty.
*Dotty who?*
Dotty way the cookie crumbles.

Knock, knock.
*Who's there?*
Yukon.
*Yukon who?*
Yukon lead a horse to water, but you can't make it drink.

Knock, knock.
*Who's there?*
Oily.
*Oily who?*
The oily bird catches the worm.

Knock, knock.
*Who's there?*
Opera.
*Opera who?*
Opera-tunity only knocks once.

Knock, knock.
*Who's there?*
Tibet.
*Tibet who?*
Early Tibet, early to rise.

Knock, knock.
*Who's there?*
Mary.
*Mary who?*
Mary in haste, repent at leisure.

## Literary Lines

Knock, knock.
*Who's there?*
Rita.
*Rita who?*
Rita good book, you might learn something.

Knock, knock.
*Who's there?*
Gnu.
*Gnu who?*
Gnu lamps for old!

Knock, knock.
*Who's there?*
Eve.
*Eve who?*
Eve ho my hearties!

Knock, knock.
*Who's there?*
Hoffman.
*Hoffman who?*
I'll Hoffman I'll puff, and I'll blow your house down.

Knock, knock.
*Who's there?*
Saul.
*Saul who?*
Saul the king's horses, and saul the king's men.

Knock, knock.
*Who's there?*
Bibi.
*Bibi who?*
Bibi Bibi Bunting...

Knock, knock.
*Who's there?*
Thumb.
*Thumb who?*
Thumb like it hot, thumb like it cold...

Knock, knock.
*Who's there?*
Franz.
*Franz who?*
Franz, Romans, countrymen, lend me your ears.

Knock, knock.
*Who's there?*
Ella Mann.
*Ella Mann who?*
Ella Mann-Tree, my dear Watson.

Knock, knock.
*Who's there?*
Ooze.
*Ooze who?*
Ooze been sleeping in my bed?

Knock, knock.
*Who's there?*

Toby.
*Toby who?*
Toby or not to be.

Knock, knock.
*Who's there?*
Thaddeus.
*Thaddeus who?*
Thaddeus the question.

# *In Person*

*A chance for you to try out some impersonations!*

Knock, knock.
*Who's there?*
Elephant.
*Elephant who?*
Elephant A. Sizes about being a Hollywood star.

### Mae West

Knock, knock.
*Who's there?*
Welcome.
*Welcome who?*
Welcome up and see me sometime.

Knock, knock.
*Who's there?*
Collier.
*Collier who?*
Collier self a man do you!

Knock, knock.
*Who's there?*
Warrior.
*Warrior who?*
Warrior been all my life?

*Greta Garbo*

Knock, knock.
*Who's there?*
Yvonne.
*Yvonne who?*
Yvonne to be alone.

*W. C. Fields*

Knock, knock.
*Who's there?*
Melita.
*Melita who?*
Melita chickadee.

### Bugs Bunny

Knock, knock.
*Who's there?*
Yacht.
*Yacht who?*
Yacht's up, Doc?

### Humphrey Bogart

Knock, knock.
*Who's there?*
Ears.
*Ears who?*
Ears looking at you, kid.

### Groucho Marx

Knock, knock.
*Who's there?*
Ella.
*Ella who?*
Ella Vator. Doesn't that give you a lift?

Knock, knock.
*Who's there?*
Little old lady.
*Little old lady who?*
My! You're good at yodelling!

Knock, Knock.
*Who's there?*
Beets.
*Beets who?*
Beets me, but I just forgot the joke.

Knock, Knock.
*Who's there?*
Ice Cream.
*Ice Cream who?*
Ice Cream and scream and scream until I'm sick.

Knock, knock.
*Who's there?*
Cellar.
*Cellar who?*
Cellar. No, I think she can be repaired.

Knock, knock.
*Who's there?*
Odel-lay-he.
*Odel-lay-he who?*
Didn't know you could yodel.

Knock, knock.
*Who's there?*

Juno.
*Juno who?*
Of course I do!

Knock, knock.
*Who's there?*
Hal.
*Hal who?*
Hallo to you too!

Knock, knock.
*Who's there?*
Ike.
*Ike who?*
Ike Ant stop laughing.

Knock, knock.
*Who's there?*
Statue.
*Statue who?*
Statue? This is me.

Knock, knock.
*Who's there?*
Alfred.
*Alfred who?*
Alfred the needle if you sew.

Knock, knock.
*Who's there?*
Worzel.
*Worzel who?*
It's upstairs—first on the left.

Knock, knock.
*Who's there?*
Yah.
*Yah who?*
Ride 'em cowboy!

Knock, knock.
*Who's there?*
Cook.
*Cook who?*
That's the first I've heard this year.

Knock, knock.
*Who's there?*
Toodle.
*Toodle who?*
Bye, bye!

# Sarah Doctor in the House?

Knock, knock.
*Who's there?*
Sarah.
*Sarah who?*
Sarah doctor in the house?

Knock, knock.
*Who's there?*
Ivan.
*Ivan who?*
Ivan infectious disease.
*Slam!*

*Knock, knock.*
*Who's there?*
Aileen.
*Aileen who?*
Aileen Dover and fell down.

Knock, knock.
*Who's there?*
Artichoke.
*Artichoke who.*
Artichoke when he swallowed his yo-yo.

Knock, knock.
*Who's there?*
Atch.
*Atch who?*
Nasty cold you've got.

Knock, knock.
*Who's there?*
Colin.
*Colin who?*
Colin the doctor, I'm not well.

Knock, knock.
*Who's there?*
Elke.
*Elke who?*
Elke Seltzer . . . plop, plop, fizz.

Knock, knock.
*Who's there?*

Aida.
*Aida who?*
Aida lot of green apples, now I feel sick.

Knock, knock.
*Who's there?*
Arch.
*Arch who?*
Sounds like you got the flu.

Knock, knock.
*Who's there?*
Jessica.
*Jessica who?*
Jessica than I thought. I'll get a doctor.

Knock, knock.
*Who's there?*
Atomic.
*Atomic who?*
Atomic ache.

Knock, knock.
*Who's there?*
Agatha.
*Agatha who?*
Agatha headache. Got an aspirin?

Knock, knock.
*Who's there?*
Money.
*Money who?*
Money is stiff since I knocked it on the table leg.

Knock, knock.
*Who's there?*
Stan.
*Stan who?*
Stan back, I'm going to sneeze.

Knock, knock.
*Who's there?*
Di.
*Di who?*
Di Laffin.

Knock, Knock.
*Who's there?*
Mummy.
*Mummy who?*
Mummeasles are better so can I come in?

Knock, knock.
*Who's there?*

Santa.
*Santa who?*
Santa forward in our team was ill today.

Knock, knock.
*Who's there?*
Major.
*Major who?*
Major headache, that noise.

Knock, knock.
*Who's there?*
Lee.
*Lee who?*
Lee me alone! I've got a headache.

Knock, knock.
*Who's there?*
Illegal.
*Illegal who?*
Illegals stay in the nest until they feel better.

Knock, knock.
*Who's there?*
Bless.
*Bless who?*
I didn't sneeze!

Knock, knock.
*Who's there?*
Abbey.
*Abbey who?*
Abbey stung me on the nose.

Knock, knock.
*Who's there?*
Hatch.
*Hatch who?*
God bless you.

Knock, knock.
*Who's there?*
Myope.
*Myope who?*
Myope is that you get well soon.

# World Affairs

Knock, knock.
*Who's there?*
Europe.
*Europe who?*
Europe to no good.

Knock, knock.
*Who's there?*
Venice.
*Venice who?*
Venice your mother coming home?

Knock, knock.
*Who's there?*
Sicily.
*Sicily who?*
Sicily question to ask.

Knock, knock.
*Who's there?*
Lisa.
*Lisa who?*
Lisa you can do is let me in.

Knock, knock.
*Who's there?*
Yolanda.
*Yolanda who?*
Yolanda me some money?

Knock, knock.
*Who's there?*
Bella.
*Bella who?*
Bella not-a work so I knock-a on-a de door!

Knock, knock.
*Who's there?*
Vanessa.
*Vanessa who?*
Vanessa you going to grow up?

Knock, knock.
*Who's there?*

Isiah.
*Isiah who?*
Isiah nothing till you open the door.

Knock, knock.
*Who's there?*
Hanover.
*Hanover who?*
Hanover the money!

Knock, knock.
*Who's there?*
Harvey.
*Harvey who?*
Harvey gonna play this game forever?

Knock, knock.
*Who's there?*
Avon.
*Avon who?*
Avon who to come and open zis door.

Knock, knock.
*Who's there?*
Mitzi.
*Mitzi who?*
Mitzi door shut you'll never find out.

Knock, knock.
*Who's there?*
Weavish.
*Weavish who?*
Weavish you a merry Christmas and a happy New Year.

Knock, knock.
*Who's there?*
Sophie.
*Sophie who?*
Sophie come to the end of the lesson.

Knock, knock.
*Who's there?*
Weevil.
*Weevil who?*
Weevil only be staying a minute.

Knock, knock.
*Who's there?*
Veal chop.
*Veal chop who?*
Veal chop around and see what bargains vee can pick up.

Knock, knock.
*Who's there?*
Dwayne.
*Dwayne who?*
Dwayne in Spain falls mainly on the plain.

Knock, knock.
*Who's there?*
Valencia.
*Valencia who?*
Valencia dollar when will I get it back?

Knock, knock.
*Who's there?*
Marcella.
*Marcella who?*
Marcella's full of water.

Knock, knock.
*Who's there?*
Senor.
*Senor who?*
Senor mother out and let me in.

Knock, knock.
*Who's there?*
Juanita.
*Juanita who?*
Juanita 'nother hot dog?

Knock, knock.
*Who's there?*
Don Giovanni.
*Don Giovanni who?*
Don Giovanni talk to me anymore?

Knock, knock.
*Who's there?*
Don Juan.
*Don Juan who?*
Don Juan to go out today?

Knock, knock.
*Who's there?*
Don Juan.
*Don Juan who?*
Don Juan to stay out here forever?

Knock, knock.
*Who's there?*

Signor.
*Signor who?*
Signor light on, so I knocked.

Knock, knock.
*Who's there?*
Summertime.
*Summertime who?*
Summertime you can be a big pest.

Knock, knock.
*Who's there?*
Francis.
*Francis who?*
Francis the other side of the English Channel.

Knock, knock.
*Who's there?*
Francis.
*Francis who?*
Francis where people speak French.

Knock, knock.
*Who's there?*
Monkey.
*Monkey who?*
Monkey won't fit, that's why I can't get in.

Knock, knock.
*Who's there?*
Oslo.
*Oslo who?*
Oslo down. What's the hurry?

Knock, knock.
*Who's there?*
Ireland.
*Ireland who?*
Ireland you some money if you promise to pay me back.

Knock, knock.
*Who's there?*
Irish.
*Irish who?*
Irish you would come out and play with me.

Knock, knock.
*Who's there?*
Diesel.
*Diesel who?*
Diesel be your bags on the step I suppose?

Knock, knock.
*Who's there?*

Otis.
*Otis who?*
Otis a wonderful day for a walk in the park.

Knock, knock.
*Who's there?*
Ottawa.
*Ottawa who?*
Ottawa know you're telling the truth?

Knock, knock.
*Who's there?*
Havana.
*Havana who?*
Havana wonderful time, wish you were here.

Knock, knock.
*Who's there?*
Cantaloupe.
*Cantaloupe who?*
Cantaloupe with you tonight.

Knock, knock.
*Who's there?*
Egypt.
*Egypt who?*
Egypt a bit off my best china plate.

Knock, knock.
*Who's there?*
Abyssinia.
*Abyssinia who?*
Abyssinia when I get back.

Knock, knock.
*Who's there?*
Quebec.
*Quebec who?*
Quebec to the back of the line.

Knock, knock.
*Who's there?*
Alaska.
*Alaska who?*
Alaska my mommy.

Knock, knock.
*Who's there?*
Russian.
*Russian who?*
Russian about makes me tired.

Knock, knock.
*Who's there?*

Armenia.
*Armenia who?*
Armenia every word I say.

Knock, knock.
*Who's there?*
Indonesia.
*Indonesia who?*
I look at you and I get weak Indonesia.

Knock, knock.
*Who's there?*
Asia.
*Asia who?*
Asia going to invite me in?

Knock, knock.
*Who's there?*
Iran.
*Iran who?*
Iran away when you answered before.

Knock, knock.
*Who's there?*
India.
*India who?*
India good old summertime.

Knock, knock.
*Who's there?*
Bolivia.
*Bolivia who?*
Bolivia me, I know what I'm talking about.

Knock, knock.
*Who's there?*
Jamaica.
*Jamaica who?*
Jamaica mistake?

Knock, knock.
*Who's there?*
Huron.
*Huron who?*
Huron time for once.

Knock, knock.
*Who's there?*
Ann.
*Ann who?*
Ann Tarctic.

Knock, knock.
*Who's there?*
Amazon.
*Amazon who?*
Amazon of a bishop. What's your father do?

Knock, knock.
*Who's there?*
Amana.
*Amana who?*
Amana very bad mood.

## Tarzan Stripes Forever

Knock, knock.
*Who's there?*
Tarzan.
*Tarzan who?*
Tarzan Stripes Forever.

Knock, knock.
*Who's there?*
Llama.
*Llama who?*
Llama Yankee Doodle Dandy.

Knock, knock.
*Who's there?*
Cereal.
*Cereal who?*
Cereal pleasure to meet you.

Knock, knock.
*Who's there?*
Sherwood.
*Sherwood who?*
Sherwood like to meet you.

Knock, knock.
*Who's there?*
Alpaca.
*Alpaca who?*
Alpaca picnic lunch.

Knock, knock.
*Who's there?*
Arizona.
*Arizona who?*
Arizona room for one of us.

Knock, knock.
*Who's there?*

Ida.
*Ida who?*
It's not Ida who, it's Idaho.

Knock, knock.
*Who's there?*
Kentucky.
*Kentucky who?*
Kentucky come out to play?

Knock, knock.
*Who's there?*
Louisiana.
*Louisiana who?*
Louisiana boyfriend broke up.

Knock, knock.
*Who's there?*
Minneapolis.
*Minneapolis who?*
Minneapolis a day keeps the doctor away.

Knock, knock.
*Who's there?*
Nantucket.
*Nantucket who?*
Nantucket, but she'll have to give it back.

Knock, knock.
*Who's there?*
Zippy.
*Zippy who?*
Mrs. Zippy.

Knock, knock.
*Who's there?*
Nevada.
*Nevada who?*
Nevada saw you look worse, you should be in bed.

Knock, knock.
*Who's there?*
Tennessee.
*Tennessee who?*
Tennessee you tonight?

Knock, knock.
*Who's there?*
Tucson.
*Tucson who?*
Tucson an' two daughters are enough kids.

Knock, knock.
*Who's there?*
Utah.

*Utah who?*
Utah sight, utah mind.

Knock, knock.
*Who's there?*
Utah.
*Utah who?*
Utah the road and I'll mend the fence.

Knock, knock.
*Who's there?*
Yukon.
*Yukon who?*
Yukon go away and come back at a reasonable time.

Knock, knock.
*Who's there?*
Yukon.
*Yukon who?*
Yukon say that again.
Okay. I will. Knock, knock.
*Who's there?*
Yukon.
(Repeat over and over.)

# I Didn't Come Here to be Insulted!

Knock, knock.
*Who's there?*
Cook.
*Cook who?*
Cuckoo yourself! I didn't come here to be insulted!

Knock, knock.
*Who's there?*
Al.
*Al who?*
Al go home if you're not nice to me.

Knock, knock.
*Who's there?*
Gopher.
*Gopher who?*
Gopher a long walk off a short pier.

Knock, knock.
*Who's there?*
Dummy.
*Dummy who?*
Dummy a favor and get lost.

Knock, knock.
*Who's there?*
Sir.
*Sir who?*
Sir View right!

Knock, knock.
*Who's there?*
Frank.
*Frank who?*
Frank Lee, I don't care.

Knock, knock.
*Who's there?*
Hugo.
*Hugo who?*
Hugo jump in the lake.

Knock, knock.
*Who's there?*
Urchin.
*Urchin who?*
Urchin is pointed!

Knock, knock.
*Who's there?*
Howard.
*Howard who?*
Howard you like a punch on the nose?

Knock, knock.
*Who's there?*
Ogre.
*Ogre who?*
Ogre take a running
                    jump.

Knock, knock.
*Who's there?*
Cash.
*Cash who?*
I didn't realize you were some kind of nut.

Knock, knock.
*Who's there?*

Pecan.
*Pecan who?*
Pecan somebody your own size.

Knock, knock.
*Who's there?*
Watson.
*Watson who?*
Watson your head?

Knock, knock.
*Who's there?*
Poker.
*Poker who?*
Poker and see if she's awake.

Knock, knock.
*Who's there?*
Danielle.
*Danielle who?*
Danielle at me, it's not my fault.

Knock, knock.
*Who's there?*
Orson.
*Orson who?*
Stop Orson around and let me in.

Knock, knock.
*Who's there?*
Closure.
*Closure who?*
Closure mouth, I'm talking.

Knock, knock.
*Who's there?*
Scott.
*Scott who?*
Scott nothing to do with you.

Knock, knock.
*Who's there?*
Water-skier.
*Water-skier who?*
Water-skier Dof? It won't hurt you.

Knock, knock.
*Who's there?*
Enid.
*Enid who?*
Enid spanking for being so rude.

Knock, knock.
*Who's there?*

Boo.
*Boo who?*
No need to cry—it's only a joke.

Knock, knock.
*Who's there?*
William.
*William who?*
William mind your own business!

Knock, knock.
*Who's there?*
Ida.
*Ida who?*
Ida face, she's so ugly!

Knock, knock.
*Who's there?*
Hawaii.
*Hawaii who?*
Fine, until you showed up.

Knock, knock.
*Who's there?*
Water.
*Water who?*
Water be ashamed of yourself!

Knock, knock.
*Who's there?*
Thayer.
*Thayer who?*
Thayer thorry.

Knock, knock.
*Who's there?*
Tomorr.
*Tomorr who?*
Got a speech impediment?

Knock, knock.
*Who's there?*
Acid.
*Acid who?*
Acid-own and be quiet!

Knock, Knock.
*Who's there?*
Fatso.
*Fatso who?*
Fatso matter with you?

# More Knock Knocks

Knock, knock.
*Who's there?*
Ears.
*Ears who?*
Ears some more knock knock jokes for you.

Knock, knock.
*Who's there?*
Hosanna.
*Hosanna who?*
Hosanna Claus gets down the chimney I'll never know.

Knock, knock.
*Who's there?*
Ketchup.
*Ketchup who?*
Ketchup with me and I'll tell you.

Knock, knock.
*Who's there?*
Mary,
*Mary who?*
Mary Christmas.

Knock, knock.
*Who's there?*
Rabbit.
*Rabbit who?*
Rabbit up nicely, it's a present.

Knock, knock.
*Who's there?*
Noel.
*Noel who?*
Noel E. Phant is going to poke his trunk in my business.

Knock, knock.
*Who's there?*
Dunce.
*Dunce who?*
Dunce A. another word.

Knock, knock.
*Who's there?*
Kojak.
*Kojak who?*
Kojak up the car, I've got a flat tire.

Knock, knock.
*Who's there?*
Spider.
*Spider who?*
Spider when she thought I wasn't looking.

Knock, knock.
*Who's there?*
Blue.
*Blue who?*
Blue your nose.

Knock, knock.
*Who's there?*
Lucinda.
*Lucinda who?*
Lucinda sky with diamonds.

Knock, knock.
*Who's there?*
Spook.
*Spook who?*
Spook-etti.

Knock, knock.
*Who's there?*
Socket.
*Socket who?*
Socket to me.

Knock, knock.
*Who's there?*
Pasture.
*Pasture who?*
Pasture bedtime isn't it?

Knock, knock.
*Who's there?*
Xavier.
*Xavier who?*
Xavier money for a rainy day.

Knock, knock.
*Who's there?*

Ivan.
*Ivan who?*
It's not Ivan who, it's Ivanhoe.

Knock, knock.
*Who's there?*
Whistle.
*Whistle who?*
Whistle be going home soon.

Knock, knock.
*Who's there?*
Arthur.
*Arthur who?*
Arthur any cookies left?

Knock, knock.
*Who's there?*
Juno.
*Juno who?*
Juno what time it is?

Knock, knock.
*Who's there?*
Avenue.
*Avenue who?*
Avenue heard the good news?

Knock, knock.
*Who's there?*
Minerva.
*Minerva who?*
Minerva Zereckt from all these questions.

Knock, knock.
*Who's there?*
Watson.
*Watson who?*
Watson television tonight?

Knock, knock.
*Who's there?*
July.
*July who?*
July to me about stealing my pencil?

Knock, knock.
*Who's there?*
Walrus.
*Walrus who?*
Why do you walrus ask that silly question?

Knock, knock.
*Who's there?*

Waiter.
*Waiter who?*
Waiter minute while I tie my shoelaces.

Knock, knock.
*Who's there?*
Sacha.
*Sacha who?*
Sacha lot of questions.

Knock, knock.
*Who's there?*
Moose.
*Moose who?*
Moose you be so nosey?

Knock, knock.
*Who's there?*
Alex.
*Alex who?*
Alex the questions, if you don't mind.

Knock, knock.
*Who's there?*
Noah.
*Noah who?*
Noah good place to eat?

Knock, knock.
*Who's there?*
Canoe.
*Canoe who?*
Canoe come out to play?

Knock, knock.
*Who's there?*
I don't know.
*I don't know who?*
I told you I don't know. Why don't you believe me?

Knock, knock.
*Who's there?*
Ivan.
*Ivan who?*
*Ivanhoe*, by Sir Walter Scott.

Knock, knock.
*Who's there?*
Thatcher.
*Thatcher who?*
Thatcher could get away with it.

Knock, knock.
*Who's there?*
Midas.

*Midas who?*
Midas well relax. I'm not going anywhere.

Knock, knock.
*Who's there?*
Earl.
*Earl who?*
Earl be glad to get to bed, I'm tired.

Knock, knock.
*Who's there?*
Jaguar.
*Jaguar who?*
Jaguar nimble, Jaguar quick...

Knock, knock.
*Who's there?*
Teacher.
*Teacher who?*
Teacher to go knocking on my door in the middle of the
    night.

Knock, knock.
*Who's there?*
Minnie.
*Minnie who?*
No, not Minniewho—Minniehaha.

Knock, knock.
*Who's there?*
Wheel barrow.
*Wheel barrow who?*
Wheel barrow some money and go on a trip.

Knock, knock.
*Who's there?*
Dewey.
*Dewey who?*
Dewey have to listen to anymore knock knock jokes?

Knock, knock.
*Who's there?*
Hubbard.
*Hubbard who?*
Hubbard can sing louder than my bird.

Knock, knock.
*Who's there?*
Aunt Lou.
*Aunt Lou who?*
Aunt Lou tired of knocking on this door?

Knock, knock.
*Who's there?*
Harmony.
*Harmony who?*
Harmony knock knock jokes do you expect me to know?

Knock, knock.
*Who's there?*
Handsome.
*Handsome who?*
Handsome candy through the door and I'll tell you more.

Knock, knock.
*Who's there?*
Atlas.
*Atlas who?*
Atlas it's Friday, the weekend's here.

Knock, knock.
*Who's there?*
Sofa.
*Sofa who?*
Sofa we haven't made any mistakes.

Knock, knock.
*Who's there?*
Butcher.
*Butcher who?*
Butcher money were your mouth is.

Knock, knock.
*Who's there?*
Lion.
*Lion who?*
Lion on your doorstep, open up!

Knock, knock.
*Who's there?*
Kent.
*Kent who?*
Kent you guess who it is?

Knock, knock.
*Who's there?*
Thumping.
*Thumping who?*
Thumping green and slimy is climbing up your neck.

Knock, knock.
*Who's there?*
Sid.
*Sid who?*
Sid down and I'll make you a nice cup of tea.

Knock, knock.
*Who's there?*
Snow.
*Snow who?*
Snow good asking me—I don't know.

Knock, knock.
*Who's there?*
Pollyanna.
*Pollyanna who?*
Pollyanna bad kid when you get to know her.

Knock, knock.
*Who's there?*
Juicy.
*Juicy who?*
Juicy that rude sign on the door?

Knock, knock.
*Who's there?*
Halibut.
*Halibut who?*
Halibut letting me in on the secret?

Knock, knock.
*Who's there?*
Weirdo.
*Weirdo who?*
Weirdo you think you're going?

Knock, knock.
*Who's there?*
Voodoo.
*Voodoo who?*
Voodoo you think you are, Superman?

Knock, knock.
*Who's there?*
Dustin Hoffman.
*Dustin Hoffman who?*
Dustin Hoffman welcome mat for you.

Knock, knock.
*Who's there?*
Lloyd.

*Lloyd who?*
He Lloyd to me, he said it was Wednesday and it's only
    Tuesday!

Knock, knock.
*Who's there?*
Derek.
*Derek who?*
Derek of the Hesperus is a famous poem by Longfellow.

Knock, knock.
*Who's there?*
Wilson.
*Wilson who?*
Wilson be there.

Knock, knock.
*Who's there?*
Conan.
*Conan who?*
Conan Jimmies go well with ice cream.

Knock, knock.
*Who's there?*
Old King Cole.
*Old King Cole who?*
Old King Cole, so turn the heat up.

Knock, knock.
*Who's there?*
Four eggs.
*Four eggs who?*
Four eggs ample.

Knock, knock.
*Who's there?*
Gopher.
*Gopher who?*
Gopher your gun, Sheriff.

Knock, knock.
*Who's there?*
Ada.
*Ada who?*
First Ada Kit.

Knock, knock.
*Who's there?*
Eskimo.
*Eskimo who?*
Eskimo questions, I'll tell you no lies.

Knock, knock.
*Who's there?*
Harold.

*Harold who?*
Harold are you?

Knock, knock.
*Who's there?*
Warner.
*Warner who?*
Warner you coming out to play?

Knock, knock.
*Who's there?*
Dino.
*Dino who?*
Dino the answer.

Knock, knock.
*Who's there?*
Granny. Knock, knock.
*Who's there?*
Granny. Knock, knock.
*Who's there?*
Granny. Knock, knock.
*Who's there?*
Granny. Knock, knock.
*Who's there?*
Aunt.
*Aunt who?*
Aunt you glad Granny's gone?

Knock, knock.
*Who's there?*
Custer.
*Custer who?*
Custer a penny to find out.

Knock, knock.
*Who's there?*
Dennis.
*Dennis who?*
Dennis says I need a filling.

Knock, knock.
*Who's there?*
Midas.
*Midas who?*
Midas well have stayed at home for all you care.

Knock, knock.
*Who's there?*
Jupiter.
*Jupiter who?*
Jupiter fly in my soup?

Knock, knock.
*Who's there?*

Arthur.
*Arthur who?*
Arthur any cats in your house?

Knock, knock.
*Who's there?*
Stu.
*Stu who?*
Stu late to ask questions.

Knock, knock.
*Who's there?*
Dozen.
*Dozen who?*
Dozen anybody want to play with me?

Knock, knock.
*Who's there?*
Howie.
*Howie who?*
I'm okay. How are you?

Knock, knock.
*Who's there?*
Candy.
*Candy who?*
Candy cow jump over the moon?

Knock, knock.
*Who's there?*
Watson.
*Watson who?*
Watson your mind?

Knock, knock.
*Who's there?*
Howie.
*Howie who?*
Howie Dewin then?

Knock, knock.
*Who's there?*
Zany.
*Zany who?*
Zany body here seen Kelly?

Knock, knock.
*Who's there?*
Athene.
*Athene who?*
Athene you in the butchers, haven't I?

Knock, knock.
*Who's there?*

Ooze.
*Ooze who?*
Ooze in charge around here?

Knock, knock.
*Who's there?*
Owl.
*Owl who?*
Owl I can say is "knock knock."

Knock, knock.
*Who's there?*
Jess.
*Jess who?*
Jess one of those things, I suppose.

Knock, knock.
*Who's there?*
Juicy.
*Juicy who?*
Juicy what I just saw?

Knock, knock.
*Who's there?*
Scold.
*Scold who?*
Scold enough for snow.

Knock, knock.
*Who's there?*
Linda.
*Linda who?*
Linda hand, I can't be expected to do it all by myself.

Knock, knock.
*Who's there?*
Caesar.
*Caesar who?*
Caesar quickly before she gets away.

Knock, knock.
*Who's there?*
Ida.
*Ida who?*
Ida terrible time getting here.

Knock, knock.
*Who's there?*
Chin.
*Chin who?*
Chin up. I'm not going to tell you any more knock knocks.

Knock, knock.
*Who's there?*

Al.
*Al who?*
Al lied.

Knock, knock.
*Who's there?*
Torch.
*Torch who?*
Torch you would never ask.

Knock, knock.
*Who's there?*
Ozzie.
*Ozzie who?*
Ozzie you later, ok?

Knock, knock.
*Who's there?*
Turnip.
*Turnip who?*
Turnip this little lane, that's where I live.

Knock, knock.
*Who's there?*
Wafer.
*Wafer who?*
Wafer a long time, but here I am again.

Knock, knock.
*Who's there?*
Cyril.
*Cyril who?*
Cyril thing—no imitations here.

Knock, knock.
*Who's there?*
Scold.
*Scold who?*
Scold enough to go ice-skating, isn't it?

Knock, knock.
*Who's there?*
Tamara.
*Tamara who?*
Tamara is Tuesday; today is Monday.

Knock, knock.
*Who's there?*
Mine.
*Mine who?*
Mine u hat just blew away.

Knock, knock.
*Who's there?*
Ivory.
*Ivory who?*
Ivory strong; how strong are you?

Knock, knock.
*Who's there?*
Major.
*Major who?*
Major answer the knock knock joke!

Knock, knock.
*Who's there?*
Lee King.
*Lee King who?*
Lee King Bucket.

Knock, knock.
*Who's there?*
Victor.
*Victor who?*
Victor his jeans getting here.

Knock, knock.
*Who's there?*
Tank.
*Tank who?*
My pleasure.

Knock, knock.
*Who's there?*
Nurse.
*Nurse who?*
Nurse sense in talking to you.

Knock, knock.
*Who's there?*
Waiter.
*Waiter who?*
Waiter I get my hands on you.

Knock, knock.
*Who's there?*
Yoga.
*Yoga who?*
Yoga what it takes.

Knock, knock.
*Who's there?*

Orange juice.
*Orange juice who?*
Orange juice sorry you asked?

Knock, knock.
*Who's there?*
Boxer.
*Boxer who?*
Boxer tricks.

Knock, knock.
*Who's there?*
Almond.
*Almond who?*
Almond your side, honey!

Knock, knock.
*Who's there?*
Trixie.
*Trixie who?*
Trixie couldn't do because he was a bad magician.

Knock, knock.
*Who's there?*
Ridya.
*Ridya who?*
Ridya bike and you'll get there quicker.

Knock, knock.
*Who's there?*
Murray Lee.
*Murray Lee who?*
Murray Lee rolling along.

Knock, knock.
*Who's there?*
Spider.
*Spider who?*
I. Spider with my little eye!

Knock, knock.
*Who's there?*
Rupert.
*Rupert who?*
Rupert your left arm in, your left arm out...

Knock, knock.
*Who's there?*
Bingo.
*Bingo who?*
Bingo'ng to come and see you for ages.

Knock, knock.
*Who's there?*
Tinker.
*Tinker who?*
Tinker bell is out of order.

Knock, knock.
*Who's there?*
U-Boat.
*U-Boat who?*
U-Boat can play with me today.

Knock, knock.
*Who's there?*
Pickle.
*Pickle who?*
Oh, that's my favorite wind instrument.

Knock, knock.
*Who's there?*
Moppet.
*Moppet who?*
Moppet up before it gets sticky.

Knock, knock.
*Who's there?*
Ohio.
*Ohio who?*
Ohio feeling?

Knock, knock.
*Who's there?*
Jester.
*Jester who?*
Jester song at twilight.

Knock, knock.
*Who's there?*
Gray.
*Gray who?*
Gray Z. about you.

Knock, knock.
*Who's there?*
Warner.
*Warner who?*
Warner a lift? My car's outside.

Knock, knock.
*Who's there?*

Witch.
*Witch who?*
Witch way to London?

Knock, knock.
*Who's there?*
Sari.
*Sari who?*
Sari I was sarong.

Knock, knock.
*Who's there?*
Moira.
*Moira who?*
The Moira the merrier!

Knock, knock.
*Who's there?*
Marmalade.
*Marmalade who?*
Marmalade me a little egg.

Knock, knock.
*Who's there?*
Thelonius.
*Thelonius who?*
Thelonius kid in town.

Knock, knock.
*Who's there?*
Button.
*Button who?*
Button in is not polite.

Knock, knock.
*Who's there?*
Pop.
*Pop who?*
Pop over to the shop for me.

Knock, knock.
*Who's there?*
Kanga.
*Kanga who?*
No, kangaroo.

Knock, knock.
*Who's there?*
Una.
*Una who?*
No I don't—tell me.

Knock, knock.
*Who's there?*

Water.
*Water who?*
Water way to answer the door.

Knock, knock.
*Who's there?*
Peter.
*Peter who?*
Peter bread and butter.

Knock, knock.
*Who's there?*
Anne Boleyn.
*Anne Boleyn who?*
Anne Boleyn alley.

Knock, knock.
*Who's there?*
Ellen.
*Ellen who?*
I've been through Ellen high water to get here.

Knock, knock.
*Who's there?*
Eugene.
*Eugene who?*
Eugene, me Tarzan.

Knock, knock.
*Who's there?*
Hanna.
*Hanna who?*
Hanna 'nother bell doesn't work.

Knock, knock.
*Who's there?*
Denis.
*Denis who?*
Denis must be the right house.

Knock, knock.
*Who's there?*
David.
*David who?*
David the doorbell, so I had to knock.

Knock, knock.
*Who's there?*
Don Harris.
*Don Harris who?*
Don Harris me or I won't come again.

Knock, knock.
*Who's there?*
Dishes.

*Dishes who?*
Dishes the very last knock knock in this book.

Knock, knock.
*Who's there?*
Hacienda.
*Hacienda who?*
Hacienda the book.

# 1,000
# Jokes for Kids
# of All Ages

# Our Dumb Friends

## (not to mention their dumb owners)

CITY BOY (visiting country for the first time): "That farmer's a magician."

COUNTRY BOY: "What—old Farmer Giles? How do you know?"

CITY BOY: "He told me he was going to turn his cow into a field."

A cat must have three tails. You don't believe me? Listen: any cat has more tail than no cat, right? And no cat has two tails, right? So any cat must have three tails!

"Dad, what has a green and yellow striped body, six hairy legs, and great big eyes on stalks?"

"I don't know. Why?"

"One's just crawled up your trouser leg!"

Rabbits can multiply—but only a snake can be an adder.

I call my dog Camera because he's always snapping.

A huge lion was roaring through the jungle when he suddenly saw a tiny mouse in his way. He stopped and snarled at it menacingly.

"You're very small," he growled fiercely.

"Well, I've been ill," replied the mouse piteously.

Did you hear about the boy who does bird impressions? He eats worms. . . .

What does a cat have that no other animal has? Kittens. . .

Harry was driving his donkey cart through the country lanes when he came to a low bridge. He got out a hammer and chisel and was chipping away at the stonework when the local policeman came riding up on his bicycle.

"What are you a-doin', Harry?" he asked sternly.

"This 'ere bridge be too low, officer," said Harry. "I can't get my old donkey through."

"You be right crazy!" said the policeman, "why don't ya dig the ground up instead of damaging the bridge?"

"Now *you're* bein' crazy," said Harry. "It's not his legs that are too long—it's his ears!"

Another country lad was being interviewed for a farm worker's job.

"You must be fit," said the farmer. "Have you had any illnesses?"

"No, sir," said the lad.

"Any accidents?"

"No, sir."

"But you walked in here on crutches," said the farmer. "Surely you must have had an accident?"

"Oh, that!" replied the lad. "I was tossed by a bull— but it warn't no accident, sir. He did it on purpose!"

Two men bought two horses at a sale in County Cork. Both the horses were very similar in appearance, so Pat said to Mike, "How shall we tell which horse is whose?"

"I tell you what," said Mike. "We'll bob the tail of one of them."

But by a mistake the tails of both horses were bobbed, so they were still in the same predicament.

"I know the answer," said Pat. "You take the white one and I'll have the black one!"

A country visitor saw a sign *Chickens For Sale*. He followed the signpost and found himself at a little country cottage. He knocked on the door and an old lady answered.

"How much are your chickens?" he asked.

"They're five dollars each," was the reply.

"Did you raise them yourself?" asked the visitor.

"Oh yes," she said. "Yesterday they were only four dollars each."

Do you know why giraffes are nosy?

Because they're always looking over walls to see what giraffe-ter [you're after].

What do you get if you cross a lion with a parrot?

I don't know: but if he says "Pretty Polly"—*smile*!

An absent-minded farmer once fed his broody hen on sawdust. She eventually laid ten eggs. When they hatched, nine chicks had a wooden leg and the tenth was a woodpecker.

A man was boasting about the number of fish he had caught in a lake.

"Mind you," he said, "they were biting easily. Why, I had to hide behind a tree to bait my hook!"

"Dad, what would happen if I stole that pony?"

"You'd go to prison, my lad."

"Oh. You wouldn't forget to feed him while I was away, would you?"

The owner of a donkey cart called the vet to a country lane.

"What's the matter?" asked the vet.

"I don't know," was the reply. "He just won't move."

"I'll soon fix that," said the vet. "I'll give him some of my special medicine."

About three seconds after the donkey had taken the medicine he went galloping off up the lane with his cart rattling behind him.

"Fantastic!" exclaimed his owner. "What do I owe you?"

"That'll be fifty cents, please," said the vet.

"Well, you'd better give me a dollar's worth or I'll never catch him!"

SMART ALEC: "How far can a dog chase a rabbit into a wood?"

INNOCENT FRIEND: "I suppose it depends on how big the wood is."

SMART ALEC: "Oh, no it doesn't. A dog can only chase a rabbit half into a wood. After that, he's chasing it *out!*"

A small girl was telling her friend all about her first visit to the zoo. "And I saw the elephants," she said, "and what do you think they were doing? Picking up peanuts with their vacuum cleaners!"

DONALD: "Mom, do you water a horse when he's thirsty?"
MOM: "That's right, Donald."
DONALD: "Then I'm going to milk the cat!"

Why does an ostrich have such a long neck?
    Because its head is so far from its body.

What did the lion say when it saw two hunters in a jeep?
    "Meals on Wheels..."

Two birds were sitting on the branch of a tree not far from a vast airport. Suddenly the calm of the summer's afternoon was broken by the roar of a jet plane screaming through the sky. As the thunderous noise died away, one bird turned to the other and said, "I bet you'd go as fast if your tail was on fire!"

"I've lost my dog."
    "Why not put an ad in the paper?"
    "Don't be silly—he can't read."

A farmer was showing a schoolboy around his farm when they came to a field where the farmer's sheep were grazing.

"How many sheep do you reckon there are?" asked the farmer proudly.

"Seven hundred and sixty-four," replied the boy after a few seconds.

The farmer gaped. "That's exactly right, boy. How did you count them so quickly?"

"Simple," said the boy genius. "I just counted the legs and divided by four!"

MAN AT AUCTION: "I've bid a great deal of money for this parrot. Are you sure he talks?"
AUCTIONEER: "'Course I'm sure. He's been bidding against you!"

FIRST FARMER: "Is that new scarecrow of yours any good, Giles?"
SECOND FARMER: "Good? I'll say so. The crows are so scared they're bringing back the seeds they took last week!"

"Why did the mother kangaroo scold her children?"
"I don't know. Why?"
"Because they ate crackers in bed!"

FIRST CAT: "How did you get on in the milk-drinking competition?"
SECOND CAT: "Oh, I won by six laps!"

A city boy was staying for the first time on a farm. The morning after he arrived, he asked the farmer if there was anything he could do to help, since he knew that there was always a lot of work to do on a farm.

"That's very thoughtful of you, my boy," said the farmer. "Yes, would you go and harness up the old cart horse for me?"

So off went the lad, full of enthusiasm. But being a city lad, he tried to put a harness on the farmer's prize bull! When the farmer eventually arrived, the poor boy exclaimed, "Oh, farmer, I've tried so hard to get the harness on him—but his ears are too stiff!"

A Scotsman paying his first visit to the zoo stopped by one of the cages.

"An' what animal would that be?" he asked the keeper.

"That's a moose, sir, from Canada," came the reply.

"A moose!" exclaimed the Scotsman. "Hoots—they must have rats like elephants over there!"

Young Chris was definitely more than a bit thick; when his pal asked him how he had enjoyed his day at the zoo, he replied, "What a ripoff! I saw a sign that said 'To the Monkeys,' so I followed it and I saw the monkeys. Then I saw another sign that said 'To the Bears,' so I followed that and I saw the bears. But when I followed a sign that said 'To the Exit,' I found myself out in the street."

"If a horse's head is pointing north, where would its tail be pointing?"

"To the south."

"No—to the ground!"

A farmer bought a new cart horse on credit; after a week he took it back to the dealer and complained.

"He does his work well enough," said the farmer, "but he won't hold his head up, and I think there must be something wrong with him."

"Don't worry about him not holding his head up," explained the dealer, "it's just his pride—he will when he's paid for!"

"I like your new dog. Is he clever?"

"I'll say! When I say to him, 'Are you coming for a walk or aren't you?' he either comes or he doesn't!"

"Who went into a lions' den and came out alive?"

"Daniel."

"Who went into a tigers' den and came out alive?"

"I don't know."

"The tiger!"

"Do you sell cat's meat?"

"Only if they're accompanied by a human being."

"I've lost my parakeet. What shall I do?"

"Notify the air force!"

A little boy was paying his first visit to the country, and his dad was taking him around a farmyard, showing him the various animals.

"And that's a Jersey," he explained.

"Is it, Dad?" asked the lad. "I thought it was a cow."

MOM: "Louisa, have you changed the water in the goldfish bowl?"

LOUISA: "No, Mom—they haven't finished what's in there yet!"

"We've got a new watchdog."

"Is he a good watchdog?"

"I'll say! The other day he stopped a dirty old tramp eating a steak and kidney pie my mom had left on the kitchen table."

"Go on!"

"He did. He ate it himself!"

All the animals in the jungle decided to form themselves into football teams and play a knockout competition. Over a period of several months, dozens and dozens of teams

played one another, until the great day dawned for the final match to decide the champion animal team. It was a fast and furious match, with thousands of animals from miles and miles around cheering and shouting with excitement.

The score was six all, and there were just five minutes left for play when Alexander the Ant went scorching down the middle. It looked as though he was just about to score when Elias the Elephant, on the defending side, squashed Alexander flat as a pancake! The referee—Claud the Camel—blew his whistle and came running over.

"You've killed him!" he said to Elias the Elephant. "That means a penalty—and I'll have to send you off."

"But I didn't mean to kill him, ref!" pleaded the distraught Elias. "I only meant to trip him!"

"My dog's got no nose."
"Poor thing! How does he smell?"
"Terrible!"

"My dog can jump ten feet."
"That's nothing—my dog can jump as high as our house."
"I don't believe it!"
"It's true, although our house can't jump very high."

OLD LADY: "Little boy, don't make faces at that poor bulldog."
LITTLE BOY: "Well, he started it!"

A man went into a pet shop to buy a parrot. He was shown an especially fine one which he liked the look of, but he was puzzled by the two strings tied to its feet.

"What are they for?" he asked the pet shop manager.

"Ah, well, sir," came the reply, "that's a very unusual feature of this particular parrot. You see, he's a trained parrot, sir—used to be in a circus. If you pull the string on his left foot he says 'Hello!,' and if you pull the string on his right foot he says 'Good-bye!'"

"And what happens if I pull both the strings at the same time?"

"I fall off my perch, you fool!" screeched the parrot.

"Have you ever seen a man-eating tiger?"

"No, but in the cafe next door I once saw a man eating chicken!"

"Have you ever seen a dog make a rabbit hutch?"

"No, but I've seen a fox make a chicken run."

Over the public address system came the following announcement: "Here is the result of today's sheepdog trials. All the sheepdogs have been found not guilty."

"Why do you call your dog Mechanic?"

"Because every time I throw something at him he makes a bolt for the door!"

The new kitten sitting by the fireside began to purr in the cozy warmth. This unexpected reaction threw little Peter into a panic. "Mom," he called, "the kitten's starting to boil!"

"Would you like to play with our new dog?"

"He looks very fierce. Does he bite?"

"That's what I want to find out."

"What's your new dog's name?"

"Dunno—he won't tell me."

"My cat took first prize at the bird show."

"Your cat took first prize at the *bird* show? How did he manage that?"

"He ate the prize canary. . . ."

A cheap horseman went into a saddler's shop and asked for one spur.

"One spur?" asked the saddler. "Surely you mean a pair of spurs, sir?"

"No, just one," replied the horseman. "If I can get one side of the horse to go, the other side is bound to come with it!"

"Would you rather a lion ate you or a gorilla?"
"I'd rather the lion ate the gorilla. . . ."

# What's Up, Doc?

DOCTOR: "You must take four teaspoonsful of this medicine before every meal."
SMALL PATIENT: "But we've only got three teaspoons!"

DISTRAUGHT MAN: "Doctor, doctor, my hair's falling out. Can you give me something to keep it in?"
DOCTOR: "How about a paper bag?"

FOOLISH MAN: "Doctor, doctor, come quickly! My wife's broken a leg!"
DOCTOR: "But I'm a doctor of music."
FOOLISH MAN: "That's all right—it's the piano leg!"

A boy had the bad luck to break a leg playing football. After his leg had been put in a cast, he asked the doctor, "When you take the cast off, will I be able to play the violin?"

"Of course you will," said the doctor reassuringly.

"That's funny," said the boy. "I couldn't before you put it on."

MOM: "Jenny, the doctor says you must take one of these pills three times a day."
JENNY: "How can I take it more than once?"

MOM: "Joe, time for your medicine."
JOE: "I'll fill up the bathtub."
MOM: "Why?"
JOE: "Because on the bottle it says 'to be taken in water.'"

A slow-thinking country lad was complaining to his friend about his illness.

"I can't keep nuttin' on my stomach. The doctor gave me some pills—but they rolled off in the night!"

The newly qualified young doctor was examining a patient.

"Have you had this before?" he asked, plainly baffled.

16

"Yes, doctor," said the unfortunate patient.

"Well, you've got it again!"

Anyone who goes to a psychiatrist ought to have his head examined...

A famous surgeon went on a safari to Africa. When he came back, his colleagues asked him how it had been.

"Oh, it was very disappointing," he said. "I didn't kill a thing—I'd have been better off staying here in the hospital!"

A doctor had just given a schoolboy a vaccination, and was about to put a bandage on his arm.

"Would you put it on the other arm, please, doctor?" asked the boy.

"What's the point of that?" said the doctor. "I'll put it over your vaccination so that the other boys will know not to bang into it."

"You don't know the kids at my school!" said the boy mournfully.

DOCTOR: "How's that bad cold of yours? Did you take a hot bath and the medicine I prescribed for you?"

PATIENT: "Well, I took the hot bath, but by the time I'd finished it there wasn't room for the medicine."

PATIENT: "Doctor, I'm afraid my wife mistook that medicine you gave me for furniture polish."
DOCTOR: "So you want me to give you some more?"
PATIENT: "No, I want you to come and shake our table."

FRANTIC PATIENT: "Doctor, I've just swallowed a mouth organ!"
DOCTOR: "It could be worse—at least you don't play the piano!"

DOCTOR: "Well, I've given you a thorough checkup, and there's not much wrong with you other than lack of exercise. What you must do is to take a brisk walk every day of not less than three miles."
PATIENT: "Oh, I'll get terribly dizzy if I do that, doctor."
DOCTOR: "Why on earth should you get dizzy walking?"
PATIENT: "I'm a lighthouse keeper."

DOCTOR: "Well now, is your cough better this morning?"
PATIENT: "It should be. I've been practicing all night."

As the doctor approached the schoolboy to give him an injection the boy yelled out loud.

"What's the matter?" said the doctor crossly. "I haven't touched you yet."

"You're standing on my foot!" answered the boy.

"My doctor's told me to give up golf."

"Why—because of your health?"

"No. He looked at my score card."

A short-sighted man went to the doctor for advice about his eyesight, and the doctor told him to eat carrots. He came back three months later to complain about the diet.

"Last night, doctor," he said, "I went out to my garden. It was very dark and I fell over."

"Couldn't you see well enough?" asked the doctor.

"Yes, I could see all right. I tripped over my ears."

PATIENT: "Doctor, doctor—I can't sleep! It's driving me crazy. I can't sleep, I tell you!"

DOCTOR: "You should lie on the edge of the bed. You'll soon drop off."

PATIENT: "Doctor, I snore so loudly I keep myself awake. What can I do?"

DOCTOR: "Sleep in another room."

DOCTOR: "What's your trouble, then?"

PATIENT: "Water on the knee."

DOCTOR: "How do you know?"

PATIENT: "I dropped a bucket full of it!"

A man had been unfortunate enough to injure his hand at work. As the doctor was examining it he shook his head and said, "I'm afraid it'll never be right."

"Why not, doctor?" asked the patient anxiously.

"Because it's your left hand," replied the nutty medico.

The vicar saw one of his older parishioners limping slowly down the street one day and said to him, "I'm sorry to see you in this state, Mr. Brown. What's the trouble?"

"It's my corns, vicar," said the old chap.

"What does the doctor say?" asked the kindly vicar.

"Haven't been to a doctor," said the old fellow stubbornly.

"Well," said the vicar, "I would see him if I were you. He'll very likely give you something for them."

"Why should I?" came the indignant reply. "They've never done anything for me. Let 'em suffer!"

DOCTOR: "Your system needs toning up. What you should do is take a nice cold bath every morning."

PATIENT: "Oh, I do, doctor."

DOCTOR: "You do?"
PATIENT: "Yes, every morning I take a nice cold bath and I fill it with nice warm water!"

A little girl attending the school clinic started crying as the doctor approached her.

"I'm only going to take your pulse," the doctor explained.

"But don't I need it?" sobbed the little girl.

DOCTOR: "Now just step on the scales. There, you see? Look at this chart—you're overweight."
PATIENT: "No, I'm not. I'm just six inches too short."

A doctor advised a very fat man to take up golf for exercise. "That's no good to me," said the patient. "I've tried it before. If I put the ball where I can hit it, I can't see it, and if I put it where I can see it, I can't hit it!"

A man at work cut his hand very badly. He was taken to the emergency room of the local hospital, where a doctor examined it and said, "I'll have to put some stitches in that."

"Right, doctor," said the patient, "And while you're at it, will you sew this button back on my shirt for me?"

A patient whose doctor advised him to get away to the seaside for a rest and a change came back after a week

and went to report to the doctor.

"Well, did the rest and the change do you good?" asked the doctor.

"Not much," said the disgruntled patient. "The doorman got my change and the hotel got the rest."

"Dr. Sawbones speaking."

"Oh, doctor, my wife's just dislocated her jaw. Can you come over in, say, three or four weeks' time?"

A plump young woman went to see her doctor.

"I'm worried about losing my figure, doctor," she said.

"You'll just have to diet," said the doctor unsympathetically.

"What color?" asked the woeful patient.

A doctor had been attending a rich old man for some time, but it became apparent that the old guy had not long to live. Accordingly, the doctor advised his wealthy patient to put his affairs in order.

"Oh, yes, I've done that," said the old gentleman. "I've only got to make my will. And do you know what I'm going to do with all my money? I'm going to leave it to the doctor who saves my life...."

DOCTOR: "Why didn't you send for me sooner, madam? Your husband is very ill."
WIFE: "I thought I'd give him a chance to get better first."

"How are you today?"
  "I'm still having trouble with my breathing, doctor."
  "Well, I must give you something to stop that."

"Doctor, come quickly!"
  "What's the matter?"
  "We can't get into our house!"
  "That's scarcely my concern, is it?"
  "Yes it is. The baby's swallowed the front door key!"

"Did you take my advice about your insomnia? Did you count sheep?"
  "Yes, I did, doctor. I counted up to 482,354."
  "And did you fall asleep?"
  "No—it was time to get up!"

"Doctor, I'm getting very forgetful."
"I see, Mr. Bloggs. Won't you take a chair?"
"Thanks—take a what?"

"A chair. Now, when did you first notice this trouble?"
"What trouble?"

"Doctor, how can I cure myself of sleepwalking?"
"Sprinkle thumbtacks on your bedroom floor."

# Lucky Dip

A small boy came into the confessional and told the priest that he had thrown peanuts into the river. The priest thought this was a strange little sin to confess to, but said nothing. The next small boy also confessed to throwing peanuts in the river, and the next. Finally a very small boy came in, so the priest said, "Did you throw peanuts in the river?"

"No, Father," said the kiddie, "I *am* Peanuts."

Can a match box? No, but a tin can.

A man asked his boss for a raise in salary. The boss said, "What do you mean? Give you a raise? You don't work here at all. Listen: there are 365 days in the year—366 this year, because it's a leap year. The working day is eight hours—that's one third of a day, so over the year that's

122 days. The office is shut on Sundays so that's 52 off, making 70 days. Then you have two weeks' vacation—take off 14 days, which leaves 56. There are four bank holidays, which leaves 52. Then the office is closed on Saturdays, isn't it? Well, there are 52 Saturdays in the year—so you don't do anything here at all. Yet you're asking me for a raise!"

As the strong man said on his way to the beach: "I'm mussel-bound!"

Did you hear about the baby boy whose father was called Ferdinand and whose mother was called Liza? They christened him Ferdilizer.

A city man was visiting the country and was praising the cleanliness of the air.

"So healthy to breathe!" he exclaimed. "No pollution like the city."

"Ar," replied a local, "I can't understand why they don't build the cities in the country!"

Two men were arranging to meet. "If I get there first I'll put a chalk cross on the wall, Tom.

"Right you are, Jim," said Tom. "And if I get there first I'll rub it off."

Did you hear about the cannibal on a diet? Now he only eats pygmies.

Do you like Kipling? I don't know—I've never Kippled.

Jeff came in the house, groaning and holding his stomach.
"Are you in pain?" his mom asked anxiously.
"No, the pain's in me!" replied Jeff.

As a large, impressive funeral was passing, a man on the pavement watching it go by asked a small boy, "Who's died?"
"The man in the coffin," said the boy.

BARBER: "How do you want your hair cut, sonny Jim?"
SMALL CUSTOMER: "Like Daddy's—with a hole in the top."

PROVERB: A pen can be driven, but a pencil does best when it's lead.

VICAR (to new choirboy): "And what might your name be, little man?"

CHOIRBOY: "It might be Cedric—but it ain't."

WANTED: Camera stand for photographer with three legs. Young assistant to club manager.

"Hey, you've got your hat on back to front."

"Mind your own business. How do you know which way I'm going?"

A wife woke her husband up one night and whispered urgently, "Alf! Alf! I was woken up by noises downstairs. I went down, and there's a burglar in the kitchen eating my fresh-baked apple pie. Call 911!"

"Who shall I ask for?" said Alf sleepily. "Police or ambulance?"

"Stop the bus. An old lady's just fallen off!"

"It's all right, sir. She's paid her fare."

An old lady caught two little boys with a packet of cigarettes and decided to frighten them into giving up cigarettes for life.

28

"Now listen to me," she said sternly. "Do you know where little boys go when they smoke?"

"Yes, lady," said the elder of the boys, "behind the church."

Overheard in a British court:
WITNESS: ". . . He was as drunk as a judge."
JUDGE: "Don't you mean 'as drunk as a lord'?"
WITNESS: "Yes, my lord . . ."

"My friend fell from a window twenty stories up yesterday."

"Was he badly hurt?"

"No—he fell inside."

FAT MAN ON BUS (to schoolboy): "Why don't you be a gentleman and give a lady your seat?"
SCHOOLBOY: "Why don't *you* be a gentleman and give *two* ladies your seat?"

## What's the difference between

—*a watchmaker and a sailor?*
  One sees over watches and the other watches over seas.

*—a lighthouse keeper, a thief, and a pot of glue?*

One watches over seas, one seizes watches. And the pot of glue? Ah, that's where you get stuck.

*—an elephant and a mailbox?*

You don't know? Then it's no good sending you to mail a letter, is it?

*—an Indian elephant and an African elephant?*

About three thousand miles.

*—maximum and minimum?*

Maxie's a boy and Minnie's a girl.

Has it struck you that no matter how short girls' skirts get, they'll always be above two feet?

*Do you know the story of the three wells?* No? Well, well, well . . .

*Do you know the story of the three eggs?* No? Two [too] bad . . .

*Do you know the story of the empty glass?* No? There's nothing in it. . . .

*Do you know the story of the dirty window?* No? You wouldn't see through it. . . .

*Do you know the story of the three deer?* No? Dear, dear, dear . . .

FRESH BOY (in shop): "Have you got any ice cream left, mister?"
SHOPKEEPER: "Yes."
FRESH BOY: "Well, you shouldn't make so much."
FRESH BOY (in another shop): "Do you have any broken crackers?"
SHOPKEEPER: "Yes."
FRESH BOY: "Well, you shouldn't be so clumsy."

A little boy went into a candy store and asked for a penny's worth of gumballs. The jar containing the gumballs was kept on the very top shelf, so the shopkeeper had to get a little ladder, climb up, get the jar, climb down, measure out a penny's worth, then climb back up the ladder to replace the jar.

Just as he had descended the ladder, another boy came into the shop and also asked for a penny's worth of gumballs. Again the shopkeeper had to go up the ladder, down the ladder, measure out a penny's worth, and then go up and down the ladder again.

In came a third boy—he also wanted a penny's worth of gumballs. And a fourth. By this time, the shopkeeper was getting exhausted, so when the fifth boy came in while he was at the top of the ladder, he said, "I suppose you want a penny's worth of gumballs, too?"

"No, I don't," said the boy.

So the shopkeeper put the jar on the shelf and came down again.

"What *do* you want then, sonny?" he asked, panting hard.

"Two cents' worth of gumballs," said the lad.

"Who was that at the door?"
"A man with a drum."
"Tell him to beat it."

"Who was that at the door?"
"The Invisible Man."
"Tell him I can't see him."

"Who was that at the door?"
"A man with a wooden leg."
"Tell him to hop it."

"Who was that at the door?"
  "A man with a trumpet."
  "Tell him to blow."

"Who was that at the door?"
  "A woman with a carriage."
  "Tell her to push off."

"Who was that at the door?"
  "A man selling beehives."
  "Tell him to buzz off."

If you're good in this life you will merit everlasting bliss—if not you'll merit an everlasting blister.

CHEAP MAN: "How much for a haircut?"
BARBER: "Forty cents."
CHEAP MAN: "How much for a shave?"
BARBER: "Thirty cents."
CHEAP MAN: "Okay—shave my head."

This story is about a man from one of the remotest parts of England where there is still no electricity or gas. For

the first time in his life he left his village and went to visit London. When he returned, his friends asked him how he had enjoyed himself.

"Well, the trouble was I couldn't sleep," he told them.

"Why was that, Harry?"

"The light was on in my bedroom all the time."

"Why didn't you blow it out, then?"

"I tried to—but it was inside a little glass bottle."

A country boy on one of his rare visits to the market town saw a music stool in the window of a shop. He went in, bought it, and took it home. Two weeks later he was back at the shop in a furious rage.

"I been sittin' on this stupid stool for two weeks," he told the manager, "an I ain't got a note out of it yet!"

FRED: "Are you trying to make a fool out of me?"
JACK: "Oh, no, I never interfere with nature."

Why is it that no matter who the buyer is, coal always gets delivered to the cellar [seller]?

LARRY: "What's the greatest race on earth?"
MIKE: "The Derby?"
LARRY: "No."

MIKE: "The Grand National?"

LARRY: "No."

MIKE: "I give up. What *is* the greatest race in the world?"

LARRY (laughing): "The human race!"

MIKE: "I don't know why you're laughing. You're not in it!"

BOY (at dentist's): "Oh, I wish we were born without teeth."

DENTIST: "We usually are!"

As one ghost said to the other ghost: "I'm sorry, but I simply don't believe in people. . . ."

A boastful American from Texas was being shown the sights of London by a taxi driver.

"What's that building there?" asked the Texan.

"That's the Tower of London, sir," replied the taxi driver.

"We can put up buildings like that in two weeks," drawled the Texan.

A little while later he said, "And what's that building we're passing now?"

"That's Buckingham Palace, sir, where the Queen lives."

"Is that so?" said the Texan. "Do you know back in Texas we could put up a place like that in a week?"

A few minutes later they were passing Westminster Abbey. The American again asked, "Hey, cabby, what's

that building over there?"

"I'm afraid I don't know, sir," replied the taxi driver. "It wasn't there this morning!"

A passerby saw a small boy reaching up and trying to ring a doorbell. He stopped and rang the bell for the boy.

"Thanks, mister," said the rascal. "Now we'd both better run for it!"

CRAFTY BOY (in shop): "How much for these toy soldiers?"
SHOPKEEPER: "Fifteen cents for two. Ten cents for one."
CRAFTY BOY: "Here's a nickel—I'll have the other one."

HAUGHTY WOMAN: "Little girl, I'm looking for a small brown dog with one eye."
SAUCY GIRL: "If he's only small you'd better use two eyes!"

So you want to play the banjo? Why pick on that?

WANTED: Strong boy for bottling.
Cottage for family with good drainage.
Room for gent, with south view and good ventilation.

Woman to wash and iron and milk three cows.
Mattress by a gentleman stuffed with horsehair.

A man stood up in a crowded restaurant and shouted, "Anybody lost a roll of five-dollar bills with a rubber band around them?"

There was a rush of people claiming to be the loser. The first to arrive was an old tramp.

"Here you are," said the man, "I've found your rubber band!"

VICAR: "How old are you, Mark?"
MARK: "Nine, vicar."
VICAR: "And what are you going to be?"
MARK: "Ten, vicar."

ROMANCE GONE WRONG
"Your teeth are like the stars. . . . They come out at night!"
"Your ears are like petals . . . bicycle pedals!"

Two boys went fishing one summer's morning and trespassed onto the rich man's land. The gamekeeper spotted them and came running up.

"Didn't you see that notice?" he roared.

"Yes," said the quick-witted boy of the two, "but it said 'Private' at the top, so I didn't want to read any further."

A city boy was taken to the country and saw a horse for the first time. "Where's his rockers?" he demanded.

CHRIS: "Hello, Colin. I like your tie. I bet I know where you got it."

COLIN: "All right, then, smartie. Where?"

CHRIS: "Around your neck!"

COLIN: "Never mind my tie. I was in the supermarket this morning with mom and there was a man with no trousers on."

CHRIS: "Was he arrested?"

COLIN: "No—he was wearing shorts!"

CHRIS: "Very funny—ha, ha! My mom took me to the movies last night."

COLIN: "Oh, did she? Did you like it?"

CHRIS: "No, I cried."

COLIN: "Why, was it sad?"

CHRIS: "Dunno—we couldn't get in!"

COLIN: "My mom took me to the cemetery this afternoon."

CHRIS: "Oh—anyone dead?"

COLIN: "Yes—all of 'em!"

An angel in heaven was welcoming a new arrival. "How did you get here?" he asked.

And the new angel replied, "'Flu..."

A man who always slept with his mouth open woke up his wife in a fright one night.

"What is it?" she said.

"I've just swallowed a mouse!" cried the husband. "What should I do?"

"Don't worry," said his wife. "I'll tie a piece of cheese to your nose, then the mouse will come out."

So she did just this and went back to sleep. But an hour later her husband was waking her up again, even more panic-stricken.

"What is it this time?" she demanded.

"I've just swallowed the cat!"

JENNY: "I haven't slept for days."
SARAH: "Why not?"
JENNY: "I sleep at night."

*Extract from a reply to an advertisement:* "I am replying to your advertisement for an organist and chorus master, either lady or gentleman. I have been both for many years. . . ."

The proud owner of an impressive new clock was showing it off to a friend.

"This clock," he said, "will go for fourteen days without winding."

"Really?" replied his friend. "And how long will it go if you do wind it?"

MOM: "You can't come in unless your feet are clean."
SMALL BOY: "They are clean, Mom. It's only my shoes that are dirty."

CHARLIE: "I bet I know where you're going tonight."
SADIE: "All right, then, smart guy. Where am I going tonight?"
CHARLIE: "To sleep."

A man who moved into a new house called it "Simla." A friend visited him and asked, "Why do you call your house Simla. Were you in India?"

"No," the owner replied, "it's just that it's *sim'lar* to all the other houses in the street!"

A kind-hearted old lady saw a little girl standing in the park crying.

"What's the matter, dear?" she asked.

"Rheumatism," was the unexpected reply.

"Rheumatism?" exclaimed the old lady. "At your age?"

"No," sobbed the little girl, "I can't spell it!"

A man went to the optician to have his eyes tested. The optician sat him down and showed him a test card.

"Can you read that?" asked the optician.

"No," said the man.

The optician moved it closer: "Now can you read it?"

"No," said the man.

The optician moved the chart even closer: "Surely you can read it now?"

"No," said the man. "I can't read."

"Are you hungry?"

"Yes, Siam."

"Come on, I'll Fiji."

"I bet I can make you speak like a Red Indian."

"How?"

"That's right!"

PASSERBY (to fisherman): "Is this river good for fish?"

FISHERMAN: "It must be. I can't get any of them to leave it!"

VEGETARIAN: "I've lived on nothing but vegetables for years."

BORED LISTENER: "That's nothing. I've lived on Earth all my life."

SNAKE CHARMER: "Be careful with that trunk, porter. It contains a ten-foot snake."
PORTER: "You can't kid me—snakes don't have any feet."

Harry was given two apples, a small one and a large one, by his Mom. "Share them with your sister," she said.

So Harry gave the small one to his little sister and started biting into the large one.

"Hey!" said his sister. "If mom had given them to me I'd have given you the large one and had the small one myself."

"Well," said Harry, "that's what you've got, so what are you worrying about?"

THINGS THAT
MONEY CAN'T BUY: A button for a coat of paint.
Sheets for an oyster bed.
False teeth for a river's mouth.
Music for a rubber band.
Shoes for a walking stick.
A saddle for a clothes horse!

A boy was sitting on a street corner, fishing into a bucket. A kind-hearted old lady passing took pity on him, so she gave him a quarter.

"How many have you caught today?" she asked.

"You're the seventh," said the boy smugly.

A small but saucy boy was on vacation at the shore. He went down to the beach and said to the guard, "Can I swim in the sea?"

"Yes, sonny," said the guard.

"That's funny," said the lad, "in the swimming pool at home I can't swim a stroke."

"I'm glad I wasn't born in France."

"Why?"

"I can't speak French."

As the judge said to the dentist: "Do you swear to pull the tooth, the whole tooth, and nothing but the tooth?"

NOTICE (in a shoeshop window): Boots and shoes polished inside.

"What happens if you dial 116?"

"I don't know. What?"

"A policeman comes along upside down."

MAN IN CLOTHES SHOP: "Can I try on that blue suit in the window?"

MANAGER: "No, sir, you'll have to use the dressing room like everyone else."

A man in a swimming-pool was on the very top diving board. He poised, lifted his arms, and was about to dive off when the attendant came running up, shouting, "Don't dive—there's no water in the pool!"

"That's all right," said the man. "I can't swim!"

POLICEMAN (to motorist): "I'll have to report you, sir. You were doing at least eighty miles an hour."

MOTORIST: "That can't be, officer—I've only been driving for ten minutes."

"They're not going to grow bananas any longer."

"Really? Why not?"

"Because they're long enough already."

## What's the difference between

*—a bottle of medicine and a doormat?*

One is shaken up and taken and the other is taken up and shaken.

*—a hungry boy and a greedy boy?*
One longs to eat and the other eats too long.

*—a nail and a bad boxer?*
One is knocked in and the other is knocked out.

*—a spendthrift and a pillow?*
One is hard up and the other is soft down.

*—a barber in ancient Rome and an excited circus owner?*
One is a shaving Roman and the other is a raving showman.

"My uncle's got a wooden leg."
"That's nothing. My auntie's got a wooden chest."

Did you hear about the girl who got engaged to a fellow and then found out he had a wooden leg? She broke it off, of course. . . .

**Railway station announcements:**
"Will passengers taking the six forty-five train from platform six to Philadelphia kindly put it back? . . ."

"Will the train now standing on platform one please get back on the rails?..."

"The train now arriving on platforms five, six, and seven is coming in sideways...."

CUSTOMER: "You made this suit tighter than my skin."
TAILOR: "Tighter than your skin? That's impossible."
CUSTOMER: "Well, I can sit down in my skin, but I can't in this suit!"

HELPFUL PASSERBY (to stranger): "Are you lost?"
STRANGER: "No, I'm here. It's the railway station that's lost."

As two boys were passing the vicarage, the vicar leaned over the wall and showed them a ball.

"Is this yours?" he asked.

"Did it do any damage, vicar?" said one of the boys.

"No," replied the vicar.

"Then it's mine."

A soapbox orator in Times Square finished his long-winded speech and then asked for questions.

"Come on, any questions?" he repeated, but again there

was no reply. "Someone among you must have a question," he insisted.

Eventually a little voice piped up, "I've got a question, mister."

"Yes, what is it, little boy?" said the speaker.

"If you've finished with that box you're standing on, can I have it for my Fourth of July bonfire?"

*A mail-order firm received the following cheeky letter:* Dear Sir, please send me the razor as per your advertisement in the paper, for which I enclose a check. Yours sincerely, Joe Soap.
P.S. I've forgotten to enclose the check but please send me the razor just the same.

*The mail-order firm replied as follows:* Dear Sir, thank you for your letter. We do not enclose our razor since we feel that a man with a cheek like yours doesn't need one. Yours sincerely . . .

"Just think—a big chocolate ice cream, a bag of scrumptious toffees, and a seat at the pictures for a dime."

"Did you get all that for a dime?"

"No—but just think . . . !"

"I wonder where I got that flat tire."

"Maybe it was at that last fork in the road. . . ."

TEDDY: "It's no good. I can't do it."

INSTRUCTOR: "Now, then, Teddy, you know what Napoleon said. He said, 'There's no such word as can't.'"

TEDDY: "I wonder if he ever tried to strike a match on a bar of soap."

*Road sign in an Irish country lane:* When this sign is under water, the road is closed to traffic.

At a concert, the boring singer with the tuneless voice announced, "I would now like to sing 'Over the Hills and Far Away.'"

"Thank goodness for that," whispered someone in the audience. "I thought he was going to stay all evening."

FIRST RAILWAY PORTER: "I had a terrific struggle getting a woman's trunk to the Crewe train."

SECOND PORTER: "Why, was it heavy?"

FIRST PORTER: "No. She wanted to go to Portsmouth."

A simple-minded fellow was struggling out of his house with a big table. His neighbor said to him, "Hello, Harry. Where are you going with that?"

And Harry replied, "I'm taking it to the fabric shop to have it measured for a new tablecloth."

A naughty boy was swimming in a private part of the river when the owner spotted him.

"Hey!" he bawled. "You can't swim here!"

"I'm not swimming," the lad shouted back. "I'm stopping myself from sinking!"

A man and his wife had just arrived at Heathrow Airport after an exhausting journey from the north of England.

Wearily the husband said, "I wish I'd brought the piano with me."

"What on earth for?" his wife demanded.

"I've left the plane tickets on it," he sighed.

A city lad, visiting the seaside for the first time, found himself walking along the dock of a little fishing village.

"That's the sea?" he asked an old fisherman.

"That be right, me dear," said the fisherman.

"I hear it's very good for the feet. I'd like to try it," said the innocent vacationer.

"I can help ye there, me dear," said the fisherman, and he let down a bucket into the sea, filled it, and drew it up again. "You can bathe yer old tootsies in there, me deario. Only a dime."

So the city lad paid his money, took off his socks and shoes, and had a paddle; then away he went, quite satisfied.

A couple of hours later he passed the same fisherman,

and by this time the tide had gone out quite a distance.

"My goodness!" he exclaimed. "Business must be good!"

A farmer persuaded one of his cowhands to buy two raffle tickets, for which the drawing was to be held that night at a dance. The next day the cowhand asked the farmer who had won the drawing.

"Oh, I won the first prize," said the farmer. "Aren't I lucky?"

"And who won the second prize, farmer?" asked the cowhand.

"My wife won that. Wasn't she lucky?"

"Yes, she was. And what about third prize?"

"Oh, my daughter won that. Wasn't she lucky? By the way, you haven't paid me for your tickets yet, have you?"

"No," replied the cowman. "Aren't I lucky?"

"This match won't light."

"That's funny—it did this morning."

"A noise woke me up this morning."

"What was that?"

"The crack of dawn."

"If you had two sticks, what would you do to make a fire?"

"Rub them together, I suppose."

"It's much easier if one of them is a match!"

"Do the buses run on time?"

"Usually, yes."

"No, they don't. They run on wheels."

A very fat man started taking violin lessons, and shortly afterward was stopped by a friend in the street.

"How's the violin progressing?" asked the friend.

"Oh, I've given it up," said the fat man.

"Why's that?" asked his friend.

"Well, my teacher told me to put the violin under my chin—and I couldn't decide which one!"

What did the tell-your-weight machine say when a very fat lady stepped on it?

"One at a time, please!"

"It can't go on! It can't go on!"

"What can't go on?"

"This baby's vest—it's too small for me."

"It's gone forever—gone forever, I tell you!"

"What has?"

"Yesterday."

"It's not worth two cents—I insist that it's not worth two cents!"

"What isn't?"
"A penny!"

Notice (in an undertaker's window): Press the bell if you want attention three times.

"Do you know all the buses and trains are stopping today?"
"No, I didn't. Why is that?"
"To let the passengers off."

MAN (in pharmacy): "I'd like some soap, please."
ASSISTANT: "Scented?"
MAN: "No, I'll take it with me."

"I can tell the time by the sun at any time of the year."
"Really? I can tell the time at any hour of the night."
"How can you do that?"
"I get up and look at the bedroom clock."

To Let: Room for two gentlemen 30ft. x 20ft.

# What's the difference between

—*an angler and a dunce?*
An angler baits his hooks and a dunce hates his books.

—*electricity and lightning?*
You don't have to pay for lightning. . . .

—*a flea and an elephant?*
An elephant can have fleas but a flea can't have elephants!

—*a tube and a crazy Dutchman?*
One is a hollow cylinder and the other is a silly Hollander.

—*a sick horse and a dead bee?*
One is a seedy beast and the other is a bee deceased.

—*a married man and a bachelor?*
One kisses the missus and the other misses the kisses.

## *From our bookshelf*

| | |
|---|---|
| Drunk and Disorderly | *by* Honor Bender |
| A Schoolboy's Troubles | *by* Ben Dover |
| The Cannibal's Daughter | *by* Henrietta Mann |
| On the Beach | *by* C. Shaw |
| The Broken Window | *by* Eva Brick |
| The Earthquake | *by* Major Disaster |
| British Workmen | *by* General Strike |
| The Insomniac | *by* Eliza Wake |
| The Burglar | *by* Robin Banks |
| Springtime | *by* Teresa Greene. |

POLICEMAN: "Why did you run away after you'd kicked your ball through that plate-glass window?"
SMALL BOY: "'Cause I couldn't bear to see it go through all that pane."

JENNIFER: "Are you coming to my party?"
SANDRA: "No, I ain't going."
JENNIFER: "Now, you know what the teacher told us. Not 'ain't.' It's 'I am not going, he is not going, she is not going, they are not going.'"
SANDRA: "Isn't anyone going?"

A lady was sitting in the movie theater when a man pressed past her to leave; in doing so he stepped very painfully on

her toes. A few minutes later the lady felt a tap on her shoulder. She turned—it was the same man.

"Did I step on your toes just now?" he asked.

"Yes, you certainly did!" she replied frostily.

"Ah, good," he said, "then this is my row."

ANGRY CUSTOMER: "These safety matches you sold me won't strike."

SHOPKEEPER: "Well, you can't get matches much safer than that."

BOSS (to janitor): "Are you sweeping out the office today?"

JANITOR: "No, sir, just the dust. I'm leaving the office where it is."

At one house, when the sanitation man came around to empty the bins, the occupier had overslept and forgotten to put his bin outside. The worker rang the bell and banged on the front door. Eventually an upstairs window was opened and a sleepy head looked out.

"Where's yer bin?" asked the sanitation man.

"I bin asleep," came the answer. "Where's *you* bin?"

"My brother's just opened a shop."

"Really? How's he doing?"

"Six months. He opened it with a crowbar."

"If I hadn't been in goal we'd have lost by twenty to nothing."

"Oh? What was the score, then?"

"Nineteen to nothing!"

A snob was walking around an art exhibition, when he paused. "I suppose this hideous monstrosity is what they call modern art!" he told an attendant.

"No, sir," replied the attendant, "that's what they call a mirror."

HENDERSON: "I bet I can tell you the name of your future wife."

BROWN: "Go on, then."

HENDERSON: "Mrs. Brown."

On a long bus journey, an old man was greatly irritated by the little girl sitting next to him, who kept sniffing.

"Have you got a hanky?" he asked crossly.

"Yes," she replied, "but my mom wouldn't like me to lend it to a stranger."

A lad went into a photographic shop with a photo under his arm.

"Do you do life-size enlargements?" he asked.

"Yes, sonny," said the shopkeeper.

"Well, see what you can do with this," said the lad— and plonked down a photograph of the Empire State Building!

"I'll sell you something for fifty cents that cost me a dollar and I'll still make a profit."

"What's that? It cost you a dollar, you'll sell it to me for fifty cents and still make a profit?"

"That's right."

"All right, here's my fifty cents. What is it?"

"A used bus ticket."

At a party, a magician was producing egg after egg from a little boy's ear.

"There!" he said proudly. "I bet your mother can't produce eggs without hens, can she?"

"Oh, yes, she can," said the boy. "She keeps ducks."

A new golfer was asked by a friend how he had done at his first attempt on the course.

"Seventy-two strokes it took me," said the new golfer.

"Why, that's fantastic!" said his friend.

"Yes, it wasn't bad, was it," the golfer agreed. "And next weekend I'm going to try the second hole."

A violinist in Britain went into a music shop and asked the girl behind the counter for an E string. The girl produced a box of violin strings and said lazily, "You'd better pick it out for yourself. I can't tell the 'e's from the she's."

A housewife went into a fish shop in a fury. "Those salmon you sold me yesterday were bad!" she complained.

"They can't have been," said the fish dealer. "They were only cured last week."

An angler was interrupted at the riverbank by an irate river warden.

"Can't you see that sign?" he roared. "It says 'No Fishing!'"

"And it's dead right," said the angler calmly. "I haven't had a bite all day."

BALD CUSTOMER (in barber's shop): "Is this bottle of hair restorer any good?"
BARBER: "Any good? We had one customer who pulled the cork out with his teeth—next day he had a handlebar mustache!"

"Have you ever seen a duchess?"
"Yes—it's the same as an American 's'!"

"I met a guy yesterday with very long arms. Every time he went up the stairs he stepped on them."

"Gosh! When he went up the stairs he stepped on his arms?"

"No, on the stairs."

A housewife went into a hardware shop and asked for something to help her with her spring cleaning.

"I've just the thing, madam," said the salesman. "This furniture polish is excellent. It'll do half your work for you."

"Really?" she replied. "In that case I'll take two cans!"

An old lady was considering buying a squirrel fur coat. "But will it be all right in the rain?" she asked anxiously.

"Oh, certainly, madam," said the manager smoothly. "After all, you've never seen a squirrel with an umbrella, have you?"

A man went into a tailor's shop and saw a man hanging by one arm from the center of the ceiling.

"What's he doing there?" he asked the tailor.

"Oh, pay no attention," said the tailor, "he thinks he's a lightbulb."

"Well, why don't you tell him he isn't?" asked the startled customer.

"What?" replied the tailor. "And work in the dark?"

Did you hear about that fat woman who went on a special diet? For three months all she ate was coconut milk and bananas. After three months she hadn't lost any weight—but she could climb trees!

"Do you like my new cap?"

"Yes, very nice."

"I used to wear a porkpie hat, but the gravy kept running down my ears...."

A car driver stopped in a little country town and asked a passerby for directions to the station.

"Quickest way to the station from here?" said the local. "Your best bet is to take a number seventy-three bus."

"Are you going to the football match this afternoon?"

"Yes. Are you?"

"No, it's a waste of time. I can tell you the score before the game starts."

"Can you? What is it, then?"

"Nothing to nothing."

MOM: "Sally, you've put too much postage on that letter."

SALLY: "Oh, have I? I hope it doesn't go too far, then!"

For years an old man had sold newspapers on a windy street corner. One bitterly cold day one of his regular customers said sympathetically, "Don't you ever catch cold, standing out here in all weather?"

"No, sir," replied the old man. "You see, selling all these papers keeps up the circulation."

A very shy young man went into an optician's one day to order a new pair of spectacles. Behind the counter was an extremely pretty girl, which reduced the customer to total confusion.

"Can I help you, sir?" she asked, with a ravishing smile.

"Er—yes—er—I want a pair of rim-specked hornicles... I mean I want a pair of heck-rimmed spornicles... er... I mean..."

At which point the optician himself came to the rescue. "It's all right, Miss Jones. What the gentleman wants is a pair of rim-sporned hectacles."

"You see that guy just getting out of his car on the other side of the street?"

"Yes, what about him?"

"I owe more to him than to anyone else on earth."

"Really? Who is he?"

"My landlord."

An old lady was making her very first flight in an airplane. She was highly nervous and insisted on speaking to the captain before takeoff.

"You will bring me down safely, won't you?" she asked anxiously.

"Don't worry, madam," said the captain cheerfully. "I've never left anyone up there yet."

Mr. Brown was reading his evening paper when there came a tremendous banging down the stairs. He jumped up, ran to the hall, and discovered his schoolboy son sprawled on the floor.

"Did you miss a step?" asked his dad.

"No, I caught every blessed one!" came the bitter answer.

A guard was about to signal his train to start when he saw an attractive girl standing on the platform by an open door, talking to another pretty girl inside the carriage.

"Come on, miss!" he shouted. "Shut the door, please!"

"Oh, I just want to kiss my sister good-bye," she called back.

"You just shut that door, please," called the guard, "and I'll see to the rest."

"I put Grant's fertilizer on my rhubarb. What do you put on yours?"

"Custard."

A keen gardener saw his neighbor planting razor blades in his potato patch. Ever eager to learn something new, he called over the hedge, "What are you expecting to grow Alf?"

"Chips!" was the reply.

A well-dressed man came out of a smart hotel and snapped to the doorman, "You there! Call me a taxi!"

"Certainly, sir," said the doorman politely. "You are a taxi."

At the scene of a bank raid the police sergeant came running up to his inspector and said, "He got away, sir!"

The inspector was furious. "But I told you to put a man

on all the exits!" he roared. "How could he have gotten away?"

"He left by one of the entrances, sir!"

"Can I share your sled?"

"Sure, we'll go halves."

"Gosh, thanks!"

"I'll have it for downhill and you can have it for uphill."

"I'd like a fur coat, please."

"Certainly, madam. What fur?"

"To keep myself warm, of course."

The cheapest man in Britain went into a garage and asked for a pint of antifreeze. "Certainly, sir," said the salesman. "What sort of car is it for?"

"It's not for a car. I'm going to drink it to save buying myself an overcoat this winter."

"Did you follow the doctor's diet?"

"Well, I did for a few days, then I got fed up with it. I mean, what's the point of starving to death just to live a few years longer?"

"I bought a piano twenty years ago and I still can't play it."

"Why not?"

"I can't get the lid open."

NOTICE (in a new shop window): Don't go elsewhere and be robbed—try us!

"I've taken up horse riding."

"How have you been getting on?"

"I've been taking a running jump!"

"Is your horse a good one?"

"Well, I suppose so, but he's much too polite."

"Polite? A horse?"

"Yes. Every time we approach a jump, he lets me go first."

"I hear you've just come back from India."

"That's right—I was a guest of a rajah."

"Were you really? Did you go hunting?"

"Oh, yes. One day he took me into the jungle to shoot tigers."

"Any luck?"

"Yes—we didn't meet any!"

A policeman discovered a suspicious-looking character lounging up against a doorway.

"What are you doing here?" the officer demanded.

"I live here," said the man. "I've lost my front-door key."

"Well, ring the bell, then," said the policeman.

"Oh, I did, ten minutes ago."

"Perhaps there's no one in, then," suggested the officer.

"Oh, yes, my wife and two children are in."

"So why not ring again?"

"No," said the man, "—let 'em wait!"

"You know, you always remind me of Charlie Green."

"But I'm not a bit like Charlie Green."

"Yes, you are. You both owe me a dollar."

Two housewives were looking in the window of a fish shop.

"That salmon looks nice, doesn't it, Gertie?" said one.

"That's not salmon, Elsie," said the other. "That's cod blushing at the price they're asking for it!"

"What do you think of this photograph of me?"

"It makes you look older, frankly."

"Oh, well, it'll save the cost of having another one taken later on."

"How's your snuff shop doing?"

"Oh, I'm giving it up."

"Why?"

"I'm fed up with pushing my business into other people's noses."

An irate woman stormed into the greengrocer's. "Those potatoes you sold me are full of eyes!" she complained.

"Well, madam," said the greengrocer, "you said you wanted enough to see you through the week."

"How are your violin lessons progressing?"

"Not badly at all. I've already mastered the first steps."

"I thought you played the violin with your hands."

"I got canned last week."

"What for?"

"For good."

"Good morning, sir. I'm applying for the job as handyman."

"I see. Well, are you handy?"

"Couldn't be more so. I only live next door."

FRED: "Here's a riddle for you, Bob. Why did the pigeon cross the road?"

BOB: "I don't know—why?"

FRED: "To get his old-age pension. Get it?"

BOB: "No."

FRED: "Neither did the pigeon!"

TEACHER: "Where did King John sign the Magna Carta?"

CLASS JOKER: "At the bottom."

*Why did the orange stop?*
   Because it ran out of juice.

*What's mad and goes to the moon?*
   A loony module.

*What is the longest night of the year?*
   A fortnight.

*When is a door not a door?*
   When it's ajar.

*What is it that's yellow and very dangerous?*
   Shark-infested custard.

"I once lived on water for eight months."
   "When was that?"
   "When I was in the navy."

Harry was telling his friend about his vacation in Switzerland. His friend had never been to Switzerland, and asked, "What did you think of the scenery?"

   "Oh, I couldn't see much," Harry admitted. "There were all those mountains in the way."

"How do you spell "erbert?'"

"You mean 'Herbert,' don't you?"

"No—I've got the 'h' down already."

"Did you hear about the thief who stole two-and-a-half miles of elastic?"

"No."

"He was put away for a good long stretch."

A man sitting in a barber's chair noticed that the barber's hands were very dirty. When he commented on this, the barber explained, "Yes, sir, no one's been in for a shampoo yet."

"Have you any invisible ink?"

"Certainly sir. What color?"

Two mountaineers got into difficulties, and one found himself hanging by his rope over a precipice. While his friend was vainly trying to heave him to safety, the rope began to fray.

At this the one hanging down the cliff face shouted, "What happens if the rope breaks?"

"Don't worry," called his pal. "I've got another one!"

JUDGE: "Prisoner, how do you plead? Guilty or not guilty?"

DEFENDANT: "How do I know till I've heard the evidence?"

"Why do you want to work in a bank?"

"Well, I'm told there's money in it."

A very stout old lady asked a boy scout if he could see her across the road.

"I could see you a mile away!" he said, grinning.

An extremely tall man with round shoulders, very long arms, and one leg six inches shorter than the other went into a tailor's shop.

"I'd like to see a suit that will fit me," he told the tailor.

"So would I, sir," the tailor sympathized. "So would I."

A woman called up her greengrocer to complain that although she had ordered twelve oranges, he had only delivered eleven.

"I know, madam," he agreed, "but one was bad, so I threw it away."

"Did you read about that man who invented a gadget for seeing through brick walls?"

"No."

"He calls it a window."

A certain little boy was always playing in a neighbor's backyard, much to the neighbor's irritation. One day when the boy was again rushing around in the yard making Indian war whoops, the neighbor leaned out of an upstairs window and yelled, "Didn't I tell you not to let me catch you there again?"

"Yes," called the boy, "but you haven't caught me once yet!"

"So you are applying for this job emptying gas meters, are you?"

"That's right, sir."

"Well, now, we are offering fifty dollars a week."

"Wow, do I get paid as well?"

"What did you get for Christmas?"

"A harmonica. It's the best present I ever got."

"Why?"

"My mom gives me a quarter a week not to blow it."

Did you hear about the man who's so lazy he sleeps in his garage so that he won't have to walk in his sleep?

"What sort of a car has your dad got?"

"I can't remember the name. I think it starts with T."

"Really? Ours only starts with gasoline."

"I've taken up painting professionally."

"Sell anything?"

"Yes—my car, my TV, my watch..."

"What job are you doing now?"

"I'm a debt collector."

"That's not a very pleasant job, is it?"

"Oh, I don't know. People are always asking me to call again."

"What do you mean by telling everyone I'm an idiot?"

"I'm sorry. I didn't know it was supposed to be a secret."

FIRST ACTOR: "What have you been doing lately?"

SECOND ACTOR: "Oh, I finished a film last week."

FIRST ACTOR: "That's marvelous!"

SECOND ACTOR: "Yes—and I get it back from the developer's tomorrow."

"Can I borrow that book of yours—*How to Become a Millionaire*?"

"Sure. Here you are."

"Thanks—but half the pages are missing."

"What's the matter? Isn't half a million enough for you?"

"My brother's been practicing the violin for ten years."

"Is he any good?"

"No. It was nine years before he found out he wasn't supposed to blow it."

"A pound of kiddles, please, butcher."

"You mean a pound of kidneys."

"That's what I said, diddle I?"

A lad was proudly showing his expertise on his new bicycle by racing around the block while his mom stood on the doorstep, watching him whiz past.

"Look, Mom—no hands!... Look, Mom—no feet! ... Look, Mom—no teeth!"

Did you hear about the little boy called Glug-glug? He was supposed to have been called Cedric, but the vicar fell in the font.

"Where do you think you're going?"

"To church."

"What, with dirt all over your face?"

"No, with Jimmy Green from next door."

"What do you think of my latest painting? I value your opinion, you know."

"Frankly, it's worthless."

"I know, but I'd like to hear it just the same."

FOR SALE: Alsatian pedigree dog. Eats anything. Fond of children.

*What is it that's green and hairy and goes up and down?*
   A gooseberry in an elevator.

*What has four legs and one foot?*
   A bed.

*How do you know when you're in bed with an elephant?*
   'Cause he's got "E" on his pajamas.

*Why is a small boy like a piece of flannel?*
   Because they both shrink from washing.

*Why is a pig like a bottle of ink?*
   Because it keeps going into the pen and then running out.

*What did the carpet say to the floor?*
   "I've got you covered."

*What did the big chimney say to the little chimney?*
   "You're too young to smoke."

*What did the balloon say to the pin?*
   "Hi, buster!"

## From our bookshelf

| | | |
|---|---|---|
| In the Lions' Den | *by* | Norah Bone |
| The Bank Raid | *by* | Dinah Mite |
| The Millionaire | *by* | Ivor Fortune |
| How to Cross the Road | *by* | J. Walker |
| The Jockey | *by* | Willie Winn |
| The Idiot | *by* | M. T. Nutt |
| Keeping Cheerful | *by* | Mona Lott |
| Home Heating | *by* | Arthur Mometer |
| So Tired | *by* | Carrie Mee |
| The Big Swindle | *by* | Hymer Twister |
| Aching Arms | *by* | Belle Ringer |

"How's your new apartment?"

"Okay, but it's very small. In fact, we had to scrape the wallpaper off to get all the furniture in."

"In India I used to chase wild elephants on horseback."

"Imagine that! I never knew elephants could ride horses. . . ."

"In the park this morning I was surrounded by lions."

"Lions! In the park?"

"Yes—dandelions!"

"I thought you weren't going to smoke anymore."

"I'm not."

"But you're smoking as much as ever."

"Well, that's not more, is it?"

"I bought a big book on body-building and I've been working hard on the exercises for three months."

"Is it having any effect?"

"It certainly is. Now I can lift the book!"

"What did you do in Blackpool?"

"I went to see the sea."

"Did the sea see you?"

"Well, it waved at me. . . . "

"How's your business coming along?"

"I'm looking for a new cashier."

"But you only had a new one last week."

"That's the one I'm looking for."

At the vicar's tea party for the choir, the vicar's wife had arranged a super spread with all kinds of goodies. She held out a plate to the smallest choirboy and said, "Now, then, Davey, is there any kind of cake you don't like?"

"Yes—stomach ache!" said Davey.

At the height of the battle, a message was sent down the line: *Send reinforcements. Army is advancing on the left flank.* It finally reached headquarters as: *Send three or four cents. Annie is dancing on wet planks.*

An Irishman at a fairground sat on the merry-go-round for ride after ride, getting sicker and sicker. Eventually he was positively green, so his friend said, "For goodness' sake, Paddy, will ya come off that thing! It's makin' ya ill!"

"That I will not," said Paddy, shaking but stubborn. "The feller that runs this thing owes me ten pounds, and the only way I'll get me money back is by takin' free rides on his machine!"

The cheapest man in England stopped a taxi. "How much to the station?" he asked.

"Fifty cents, sir," said the taxi driver.

"And how much for my suitcase?"

"That's five cents," said the taxi driver.

"Okay," said the cheap man. "Then take my suitcase to the station. I'll walk."

Did you hear about the very well-behaved little boy? Whenever he was especially good his dad would give him a penny and a pat on the head. By the time he was sixteen he had seventeen dollars in the bank and a flat head. . . .

As a passerby was walking under a ladder, a brick fell from a construction site and hit him on the head, ruining his new hat.

He looked up at the bricklayer and shouted, "You clumsy oaf! One of those bricks hit me!"

"You're lucky," came the reply. "Look at all the ones that didn't!"

A railway guard dashed out of the station and into a greengrocer's nearby.

"I've lost the pea out of my whistle!" he gasped. "Can you give me another one—quick!"

The greengrocer only had split peas, so the guard put one of those in his whistle and dashed back to his train.

When he blew his whistle only half of the train moved out.

"Answer the phone."

"It's not ringing."

"Why leave everything till the last minute?"

A snobbish woman was showing a friend around her new house. "It's very lovely," her friend admitted, "but what you need in this big room is a chandelier."

"I know, my dear," said her gracious hostess, "but nobody in the family plays one."

"I'll lend you a dollar if you'll promise not to keep it too long."

"Oh, I won't. I'll spend it right away!"

Auntie Gladys bought herself a new rear-engine car. She took an old friend for a spin, but after only half a mile the car broke down. Both women got out and opened up the front of the car.

"Oh, Gladys," said her friend, "you've lost your engine!"

"Never mind, dear," said auntie, "I've got a spare one in the trunk."

"Dad, Farmer Johnson caught me eating apples in his orchard."

"I've told you to keep out of there, haven't I? Did he punish you?"

"No, he said I'd been punished enough already. They were cooking apples."

"I was shipwrecked once in the Pacific and had to live for a whole week on a can of sardines."

"Goodness, weren't you lucky not to fall off!"

"Here, what have I got in my hands?"

"A horse and cart."

"Oh, you peeked!"

An angry woman swept into the butcher's shop and snapped, "That roast you sold me was awful!"

"Why, madam, was it tough?" asked the butcher.

"Tough!" said the woman. "I should say it was. Why, I couldn't even get my fork into the gravy!"

"Why are you laughing?"

"My silly dentist has just pulled one of my teeth out."

"I don't see much to laugh about in that."

"Ah, but it was the wrong one!"

A man was playing the trumpet in the street when a pal of his happened to walk past.

"I say, old chap," the friend exclaimed, "things must be tough for you if you're reduced to playing in the street!"

"Oh, I'm not hard up," said the trumpeter. "It's my landlady—she won't let me practice in the house."

"Oh, I see—do you play by ear?"

"No, I usually play over there."

"Are you superstitious?"

"No."

"Then lend me thirteen dollars."

"Next April Fool's Day we're all going to be very tired."

"Oh? Why?"

"'Cause we'll just have had a thirty-one days' March!"

"I'm going in for mountaineering."

"That's funny, I thought you always went up for mountaineering. . . ."

"My dad's an exporter."

"Is he?"

"Yes. He used to work for Amtrak."

OLD GENT (at railway station): "Porter, I want to go to Glasgow. Shall I take this train?"

PORTER: "If you like, sir—but the engine driver'll be along in a minute."

What should you do if you split your sides laughing? Run until you get a stitch in them. . . .

FOR SALE: Piano by lady with elegant carved legs.

LOST: A guitar with a green hat.

NOTICE (in a shoeshop window): Anyone can have a fit in this shop.

FAT WOMAN (getting off bus): "Conductor, this bus was very slow."
CONDUCTOR: "It'll pick up now that you're getting off, lady!"

RIVER WARDEN: "Boy! Can't you see that notice? It says 'No Swimming Here.'"
BOY: "Well, it's not true, is it? You come in and see for yourself."

"Is this a second-hand shop?"
   "Yes, sir."
   "Good. Can you fit one on my watch, please?"

A hiker stopped an old farmhand on a country lane and asked, "How far is it to Shaftesbury?"
   "Ten miles as the crow flies," came the answer.
   "And how far when he walks?" asked the hiker wearily.

A young man was being interviewed for a job. "Do you think you'd make a good bookkeeper?" asked the boss.

"Oh, yes, sir," came the keen reply. "I've sometimes kept library books for years and years."

On the ocean liner a passenger was hanging over the rail, suffering acutely from seasickness. A steward approached him to see if he could assist in any way, but the passenger just groaned and said, "Oh, I feel so ill. What shall I do?"

"Don't worry, sir," the steward sympathized, "You'll soon find out."

At an exhibition, a famous artist was asked by a gushing young lady, "Do your pictures have a big sale?"

"Only when I draw pretty boats," was the freezing reply.

FOR SALE: A cow that g ves five quarts of milk a day, a set of golf clubs, a brown overcoat, and a complete set of Shakespeare.

The nervous passenger was being reassured by the ship's steward.

"Don't worry, sir," he said. "We may be in the middle of the Atlantic, but we're only two miles from land."

"Only two miles?" queried the passenger.

"Yes, sir," said the steward. "Straight down."

A neighbor bumped into little Diana playing in the street well after dark.

"Hello, Diana," said the neighbor. "Isn't it time little girls were in bed?"

"I dunno," said Diana. "I haven't got any little girls."

---

A road worker was instructed by his foreman to dig a hole in the road.

"And what shall I do wit' the dirt?" he asked.

"Don't be silly," said the foreman, "Ya just dig another hole an' bury it."

---

A burglar, new to the life of crime, nervously held up a pawnbroker.

"Hands up or I'll shoot!" he cried.

"I'll give you twenty dollars for the gun," said the quick-thinking pawn-broker.

---

"Porter, where is this train going to?"

"This train goes to Liverpool in ten minutes, madam."

"Good gracious! Last time I went to Liverpool it took four hours."

---

A nervous young mountaineer looked up the steep cliff that his guide was proposing that they should climb.

"Do people often fall off the top?" he asked anxiously.

"No," said the guide airily. "Once is usually enough."

"Would you like a duck egg for tea?"
  "Only if you 'quack' it for me."

FOR SALE: Large crystal vase by a lady slightly cracked.

LOST: School scarf by small boy with green and blue stripes.

"Sally, how many more times have I to tell you that it's very rude to keep reaching over the table for cakes. Haven't you got a tongue in your head?"
  "Yes, but my arm's longer."

"Who are you?"
  "I'm the piano tuner, madam."
  "I didn't order a piano tuner."
  "No, madam, but your neighbors did."

"Take a week's notice. You're fired."
  "But I haven't done anything!"
  "That's why you're fired."

*Sign at the boundary to a country town*: "Corrigan welcomes careful drivers. One man is knocked down in Corrigan every thirty minutes—and he's getting mighty tired of it."

NOTICE (in a barber's shop window): Hair cut for fifty cents. Children for a quarter.

*What are hippies for?*
    To keep your leggies up.

*Why did Sir Winston Churchill wear red, white and blue suspenders?*
    To keep his red, white and blue trousers up.

*What has four legs and can't walk?*
    Two pairs of trousers.

*What goes up a drainpipe down but can't go down a drainpipe up?*
    An umbrella.

*Why is a blunt ax like coffee?*
    Because both have to be ground.

*Why do birds in a nest always agree?*
    Because they don't want to fall out.

*Why does a barber never shave a man with a wooden leg?*
Because he always uses a razor.

*What driver can never be arrested for speeding?*
A screwdriver.

*Why is honey scarce in Boston?*
Because there's only one B in Boston.

*Why is a stupid boy like the Amazon jungle?*
They're both dense.

An old man and a young boy were sitting on opposite benches in the park. Suddenly the old man leaned across and shouted, "It's no use your talking to me from over there. I'm deaf."

"I'm not talking to you," the boy shouted back. "I'm chewing bubblegum."

"Do you notice any change in me?"
"No. Why?"
"I've just swallowed a penny."

"I've just finished painting your portrait. Don't you think it looks like you?"

"Er . . . well . . . it probably looks better from a distance."

"I told you it was like you!"

Two little girls were discussing their arithmetic lessons.

"Why do we always stop our multiplication tables at twelve?" asked one.

The other had the answer. "'Cause it's unlucky to have thirteen at table," she replied confidently.

"Ticket inspector, why did you punch a hole in my ticket?"

"So you can go through, sir."

A country policeman cycling down a lane was astounded to see a hiker walking along bent under the weight of a large signpost that read, *To Plymouth*.

"Hey!" said the policeman, dismounting. "What are you up to with that?"

"I'm walking to Plymouth, constable," explained the hiker, "and I don't want to lose my way."

CUSTOMER: "I want to buy a mirror."
SHOPKEEPER: "A hand mirror?"
CUSTOMER: "No, I want to see my face."

"Are you a mechanic?"
  "No, I'm a MacTavish."

"I'm having a party next Saturday. Would you like to come?"
  "Yes! What's the number of your house?"
  "Thirty-three, Barnum Court. Just press the buzzer with your elbow."
  "Why can't I press it with my finger?"
  "Well, you're not coming empty-handed, are you?"

As a bejeweled duchess descended from her limousine, a dirty old tramp sidled up to her and said, "Excuse me, lady, I haven't eaten for a month."
  "Well, my dear man," the dowager replied, "you must *force* yourself!"

OLD LADY: "Where are you going to, my little man?"
SMALL BOY: "I'm going to the football game."
OLD LADY: "Oh, you're a supporter, are you? Is it very exciting for you when they win?"

SMALL BOY: "I don't know. I've only been going for two seasons."

LOST: An umbrella by a lady with two broken ribs.

"What's your new house like?"

"Oh, it's all right, I suppose. But my bedroom's so cold and so small—and every time I open the door the light goes on."

"Do you mind my smoking these cigars?"

"Not if you don't mind my being sick."

Inscribed on the tombstone of a hypochondriac: *I TOLD YOU I WAS ILL*.

A man rushed into a bank and stuck two fingers through the grill.

"This is a muck-up!" he hissed to the startled cashier.

"Don't you mean a stick-up?" she said.

"No," replied the bandit, "it's a muck-up. I've forgotten my gun."

Mrs. Lard, who was extremely stout, was visiting her friend Mrs. Ellis one day, when Mrs. Ellis's little girl said, "Mrs. Lard, would you get down on your hands and knees, please? Teacher says I've got to draw an elephant."

"How many fish have you caught today?"
"When I get another I'll have one."

A surly-looking tramp knocked on the kitchen door and demanded something to eat. The woman of the house was a bit frightened, but she said, "If I give you a piece of my homemade apple pie, will you promise to go away and not come back?"
"Well, you know your cooking better than I do, lady," said the tramp.

"Can you fight?"
"No."
"Put 'em up, then—you coward!"

A man went into a furniture shop and said that he wanted to buy a mattress.
"Spring mattress, sir?" asked the manager.
"No," said the customer. "One I can use all year round."

An American tourist found himself in a sleepy little country village and asked one of the locals the age of the oldest inhabitant.

"Well, sir," replied the villager, "we ain't got one now. He died last week."

"My dad's got a leading position in a circus."

"Great! What's he do?"

"He leads the elephants in."

A much-traveled explorer was talking about the huge mosquitoes of the African jungle.

"Were they vicious?" asked one of his listeners.

"No," the explorer replied casually, "they'd eat out of your hand."

A city slicker asked a farm worker the time.

"Sure, it's twelve o'clock," answered the farmer.

"Only twelve?" queried the traveler. "I thought it was much later than that."

"Oh, no, sir, it never gets later than that in these parts."

"How's that?"

"Well, sir, after twelve o'clock it goes back to one."

"You're from Scotland, aren't you?"

"Aye."

"What does 'I dinna ken' mean?"

"I don't know."

"Well, if you're Scottish, you ought to!"

"Your dad's shaved his beard off again. That's the third time this year, isn't it?"

"Yes, it's my mom. She's stuffing a cushion."

A lodger was complaining about the food to his landlady. "I didn't like that pie, Mrs. Maggs."

Mrs. Maggs was furious. "I've been making pies since before you were born!" she said angrily.

"Perhaps that was one of them," said the lodger feelingly.

A woman went into a newsstand and asked, "Do you keep stationery?"

"No, madam," said the salesman. "I usually go home for my lunch."

One housewife had a kitchen so small that she could only use condensed milk.

A guide was taking a party of visitors around a stately home. They stopped in front of a large grandfather clock and the guide said, "This clock is 350 years old, and the big hand is twelve inches long."

Before he could say another word, a little lad piped up, "If it's twelves inches long, it's not a hand. It's a foot."

"I've got a wonder watch. Only cost two dollars."

"What's a wonder watch?"

"Every time I look at it I wonder if it's still going."

"I wish I lived in olden times."

"Why?"

"There wouldn't be so much history to learn."

A tramp knocked at a kitchen door and asked for food.

"Didn't I give you some pie a week ago?" said the lady of the house.

"Yes, lady," said the tramp, "but I'm all right again now."

"What's your name, little girl?"

"Bessie."

"I know that. I mean what's your last name?"

"I dunno—I'm not married yet."

LOST: Watch belonging to a gentleman engraved "first prize."

"Can you stand on your head?"
  "I've tried, but I can't get my feet up high enough."

"I wish to return this bat. It's useless."
  "Oh? What's wrong with it, sir?"
  "Every time I've been up at bat with it I strike out."

"I saw six men standing under an umbrella and none of them got wet."
  "Must have been a big umbrella."
  "No. It wasn't raining."

A visitor to a museum was stopped at the entrance by an attendant who said, "Leave your umbrella in the cloakroom, please, sir."
  "But I haven't got an umbrella," protested the visitor.
  "Then you can't come in, sir," said the attendant. "I have strict instructions that people cannot come in without leaving their umbrellas in the cloakroom."

"How did you hurt your foot?"
  "Tim fell on it."
  "Tim who?"
  "Tim-ber."

An old lady saw a little boy with a fishing rod over his shoulder and a jar of tadpoles in his hand walking through the park one Sunday.

  "Little boy," she called, "don't you know you shouldn't go fishing on Sunday?"

  "I'm not going fishing, ma'am," he called back. "I'm going home."

"Is it difficult to get to be a professor?"
  "Oh, no. You can do it by degrees."

"I don't think much of this mirror," said the small child.
  "Why not?"
  "Well, every time I try to look at something my face gets in the way."

"I say, your umbrella's seen better days, hasn't it?"
  "Yes, it's had its ups and downs."

"What are you going to do when you grow up, young man?"

"Grow a beard so I won't have so much face to wash."

"Farmer Giles, why do you have two barrels on your shotgun?"

"So that if I miss the fox with the first I can get him with the other."

"Why not fire with the other first, then?"

A man went into the police station and put a dead cat on the counter.

"Somebody threw this into my front garden," he complained.

"Okay, sir," said the desk sergeant. "You come back in six months, and if no one's claimed it you can keep it."

"I once traveled from Edinburgh to Bristol without a ticket."

"How did you manage that?"

"I walked."

"Little girl, did you catch that big fish all by yourself?"

"No, I had a little worm to help me."

"What's a Grecian urn?"

"I dunno."

"About a hundred dollars a week..."

A tramp stopped a passerby and said, "Give me a dollar for a cup of tea, sir?"

"Tea doesn't cost a dollar!" exclaimed the outraged man.

"I know," said the tramp, "but I'm expecting company."

"Did your watch stop when you dropped it on the pavement?"

"Of course it did. Did you expect it to go right through, you fool?"

BARBER: "How would you like your hair cut, sir?"
CUSTOMER: "Off!"

A little boy knocked on the door of his friend's house. When his friend's mother answered, he said, "Can Julian come out to play, please?"

"No, I'm afraid not," said Julian's mom. "It's too wet."

"Well, then," asked the lad, "can his football come out to play?"

"If you found a dollar bill, would you keep it?"

"No, vicar."

"That's a good boy. What would you do with it?"

"I'd spend it."

"Hey! You can't fish here!"

"I'm not fishing. I'm giving my pet worm a bath."

A car driver stopped in a small village and called to a passerby, "Excuse me, can you tell me where this road goes to?"

"It don't go nowhere," said the local, grinning. "It stays right where it is."

*What is the biggest moth of all?*

A mam-moth.

*What is the biggest ant of all?*

An eleph-ant.

*What's black when clean and white when dirty?*

A blackboard.

*What orders does everybody like to receive?*
  Money orders.

*What is always behind time?*
  The back of a clock.

*What is the opposite of cock-a-doodle-do?*
  Cock-a-doodle-don't.

*Who wears the biggest hat in the world?*
  The man with the biggest head in the world.

*When is a window like a star?*
  When it's a skylight.

*When is a nail like a horse?*
  When it's driven.

*What is the longest word in the English language?*
  "Smiles"—because there's a mile between its first and
last letters.

A very pretty teenage girl said to her boyfriend, "Do you think I'm vain?"

"Of course not," he said loyally, "Why do you ask?"

"Well, girls as beautiful as me usually are."

A young man was being interviewed for a job as an office boy.

"You'll get fifty dollars a week to start off with," said the boss, "and then after six months you'll get a hundred dollars a week."

"Okay," said the lad. "I'll come back in six months."

A tramp knocked on the back door of a house and asked for a bite to eat.

"Go away," said the lady of the house. "I never feed tramps."

"That's all right, lady," said the tramp. "I'll feed myself."

The manager of a shop was bawling out one of his staff.

"I saw you arguing with a customer," he said crossly. "Will you please remember that in my shop the customer is always right? Do you understand?"

"Yes, sir," said the assistant. "The customer is always right."

"Now, what were you arguing about?"
"Well, sir, he said you were an idiot."

"Ginger, why does your bike always have flat tires?"
"So I can reach the pedals."

"Do you write with your right hand or your left hand?"
"Well, I usually write with a pencil..."

An old lady saw a little boy walking from the river with a fishing rod and a jar of minnows.

"You're a very naughty boy to go fishing on the Sabbath," she said.

"Well, it serves 'em right for chasing after worms," said the boy.

A Cockney boy was staying in the country for the first time. One evening while out for a walk with a new village friend he heard an owl hoot.

"Wassat?" he cried, startled.

"It's only an owl," said the village boy, laughing.

"I know it's an 'owl," said the town boy, "but 'oo's 'owling?"

A man climbing a cliff got stuck and called for help. When a rescue team arrived, the leader shouted to him, "Can't you get down the same way you climbed up?"

"No, I can't," shouted the frightened man. "I came up head first!"

A farmer asked his shepherd whether he had counted the sheep that morning.

"I did indeed, sir," said the shepherd. "I counted up to nineteen, but one of the creatures ran so fast I couldn't count him at all, at all."

NOTICE (in a butcher's window): John Smith butchers pigs like his father.

A fishmonger was painting *Fresh Fish Sold Here Today* above his shop when a passerby said to him, "You don't want to put *'today,'* do you? I mean, you won't be selling it yesterday or tomorrow, will you?"

"No, I suppose not," said the fishmonger.

"And then you don't want *'here'* either—you're not selling it anywhere else, are you?"

"No, that's quite right," agreed the fishmonger.

"And then why put *'sold'*?" continued the helpful man. "You're not going to give it away, are you?"

"Of course I'm not," said the fishmonger.

"And then why say 'fresh'—after all, you wouldn't sell it if it weren't fresh, would you?"

"I certainly wouldn't," said the fishmonger. "I must thank you for saving me so much trouble."

"Just one final thing," said the man. "You don't need 'fish' either—I could smell it two streets away!"

A man was spending the evening with some friends and, just as the time came for him to go, a terrible storm began, with the wind blowing at gale force and the rain coming down in sheets.

"You can't go home in this, Paddy," said his host. "You'd better stay the night."

"Thanks a million, sir," said Paddy, "that's mighty civilized of you. I'll just go home and fetch my pajamas."

Two boys were talking about the various illnesses and accidents they had suffered.

"Once I couldn't walk for a year," said the first.

"When was that?" asked the second.

"When I was a baby."

"Yesterday I saw a man fall off an eighty-foot ladder."

"Gosh! Was he hurt?"

"No, he fell off the bottom rung."

The new office boy came into his boss's office and said, "I think you're wanted on the phone, sir."

"What d'you mean, you *think*?" demanded the boss.

"Well, sir, the phone rang, I answered it and a voice said, 'Is that you, you old fool?'"

Overheard in a very crowded train: "Would you mind taking your elbow out of my ribs?"

"Certainly—if you'll take your pipe out of my mouth."

"What did you get on your birthday?"

"A year older."

A small girl went into the post office and said to the man behind the counter, "If I put a stamp on this letter, will it go to Burnley?"

"Yes, it will," said the man.

"That's funny," replied the little girl, "because I've addressed it to Plymouth."

An American tourist was visiting a quaint country village and got talking to an old man in the local pub.

"And have you lived here all your life, sir?" asked the American.

"Not yet, m'dear," said the villager wisely.

If it takes a football team forty-five minutes to eat a ham, how long will it take three football teams to eat half a ham?

It depends on whether they are professional or "am-a-chewers" [amateurs]!

# Definitions

*What is a toad stool?*
Toadstools are things that live in damp places, which is why they are shaped like umbrellas.

*What is a skeleton?*
Bones with the person off.

*What is a posthumous work?*
Something written by someone after they're dead.

*What is a buttress?*
   A female goat.

*What is a vacuum?*
   An empty space inhabited by the Pope.

*What is a net?*
   Holes tied together with string.

*What is the equator?*
   An imaginary lion running around the earth.

*What is a carafe?*
   A four-legged animal with a long neck.

*What is ice?*
   Hard water.

*What is a polygon?*
   A dead parrot.

*What is a water otter?*
  A kettle.

*What is hypnotism?*
  Rheumatism in the hip.

*What is the Cheddar Gorge?*
  A large cheese sandwich.

*What is "out of bounds"?*
  An exhausted kangaroo.

*What is an octopus?*
  An eight-sided cat.

*What is a myth?*
  A female moth.

*What is hail?*
  Hard-boiled rain.

# Keep it in the Family

## *or, blood is thicker than water (but not much)*

"Granddad, Mary Brown's mom says you're not fit to live with pigs."

"Did she now? And what did you say?"

"Oh, I stuck up for you—I said you were!"

One little boy had a very strange granny. In the winter, no matter how cold it was, she would go out and get the coal in her nightie. His dad bought her a shovel, but grannie said her nightie held more. . . .

TEACHER: "What's this a picture of?"
CLASS: "Don't know, miss."
TEACHER: "It a kangaroo."

CLASS: "What's a kangaroo, miss?"
TEACHER: "A kangaroo is a native of Australia."
SMALLEST BOY: "Wow—my big sister's married to one of them!"

A teenage girl was taking singing lessons and was practicing at home.

Her younger brother said, "Sis, I wish you'd only sing Christmas carols."

"Why?" she asked.

"Then you'd only have to sing once a year."

"Mom! There's a man at the door collecting for the old folks' home. Shall I give him Grandma?"

MOM: "If you've finished your dinner, Jimmy, say grace."
JIM: "All right, Mom. Thanks for my dinner, Lord."
MOM: "That wasn't much of a grace."
JIM: "It wasn't much of a dinner."

AUNTIE: "Do you always say your prayers, Sally?"
SALLY: "Oh, yes, Auntie, every night. I always ask God to make my baby brother a good boy—but he hasn't done it yet."

SAMMY: "Were you in Noah's ark, Grandpa?"
GRANDPA: "Er—no, Sammy, I wasn't."
SAMMY: "Then why weren't you drowned?"

Little George was crying one day, and his dad asked him why.

"I've lost a nickel," sobbed George.

"Never mind," said his dad kindly. "Here's another nickel for you."

At which George howled louder than ever.

"Now what is it?" asked his dad.

"I wish I'd said I'd lost a dime!"

Extract from a letter written by a fond mother to her son:
*Your Auntie Betty's just had her teeth out and a new fireplace put in. Well, I must write quickly now, because my pen's running out. . . .*

MOM: "I've just looked in the mirror, and I've got two gray hairs!"
EMMA: "Why's that, Mommy?"
MOM (seizing the chance): "Because you're such a bad girl to me, I expect."
EMMA: "Gosh, Mom, you must have been awful to Grandma!"

"My big sister uses lemon juice for her complexion."

"No wonder she always looks so sour."

"Was that you singing as I came in, Sis?"

"Yes, I'm just killing time before my singing lesson."

"Well, you're sure using the right weapon!"

"But don't you think my voice has improved?"

"Yes—but it's not cured yet."

A little boy was taken to a seance by his mother. The medium asked him who he would like to speak to.

"My granddad," he said.

The medium went into a trance and soon a spooky voice could be heard speaking softly in the darkened room.

"This is your granddad speaking to you, Timmy," said the voice. "What is it you wish to ask me?"

"What are you doing in Heaven, Granddad?" asked the little boy. "You're not even dead yet!"

Julie was saying her bedtime prayers. "Please, God," she said, "make Naples the capital of Italy. Make Naples the capital of Italy—"

Her mother interrupted and said, "Julie, why do you want God to make Naples the capital of Italy?"

And Julie replied, "Because that's what I put on my geography exam!"

A certain little boy had been spanked by his father one morning. When his dad came in from the office that evening, the boy called out sulkily, "Mom! Your husband's just come home."

Did you hear about the little boy who was named after his father? They called him Dad.

Another little boy's father worked away from home a good deal. In fact, he saw his father so rarely that he called him "Uncle Dad."

MOM: "Teddy, you are a naughty boy! When Billy threw stones at you why didn't you come and tell me, instead of throwing stones back at him?"
TEDDY: "Come off it, Ma. You know you can't throw for beans!"

MOM: "Sue, why did you drop the baby?"

SUE: "Well, Mrs. Jones said he was a bonny bouncing baby, so I wanted to see if he did!"

REBECCA: "Mom, did baby brother come from Heaven?"

MOM: "That's right, dear."

REBECCA: "I don't blame the angels for chucking him out!"

JOHNNY: "Dad, the vicar says we're all here to help others."

DAD: "That's right, Johnny."

JOHNNY: "So what are the others for?"

SISTER: "Boo-hoo! I made a lovely steak and kidney pie and the cat's eaten it."

BROTHER: "Never mind, Sis. Mom'll buy us another cat."

When a very important person came to the house, little Penny was allowed to take him a glass of sherry. She handed it to him and then stood there staring.

"What is it, Penny?" he asked.

"I want to see you do your trick," she replied.

"What trick is that?" asked the guest.

"Well, Dad says you drink like a fish."

**113**

DAD: "Now, son, if you're a good boy I'll give you a nice new shining nickel."
SON: "Couldn't you make it a dirty old dime?"

A mother heard her daughter giggling and whispering with her friends in the bedroom, so she called upstairs, "What are you doing, children?"

"We're playing at church," came the answer.

"Well, you shouldn't giggle and whisper in church, should you?"

"Oh, we're the choirboys."

JIMMY (boasting): "My dad once faced a snarling tiger in the jungle and didn't turn a hair."
JOHNNY: "I'm not surprised—your dad's bald!"

BUS CONDUCTOR: "Pass farther down the car, please. Pass farther down the car."
SMALL BOY: "That's not Father; it's Granddad."

DAD: "Jimmy, who gave you that black eye?"
JIMMY: "Nobody gave it to me, Dad. I had to fight for it!"

JANE: "Did you know, Mom, that the wireless was invented by Marconi?"

IGNORANT MOM: "Not Marconi, Jane; that's rude. You should say Mrs. Coni.

DAD: "Harry, how did your clothes get all torn?"

HARRY: "I tried to stop a boy from getting bashed up."

DAD: "Oh? Who?"

HARRY: "Me."

MOM: "Jimmy, you always want your own way."

JIMMY: "Well, if it's mine, why not give it to me?"

OLD LADY: "And what is your new brother's name?"

LITTLE GIRL: "I don't know. He can't talk yet."

TERRY: "Mom, can I have a quarter for an old man crying outside in the street?"

MOM: "Yes, of course. What's he crying about?"

TERRY: "Caramel apples—a quarter each."

MOM: "Sue, there were two chocolate cakes in the pantry yesterday and now there's only one. Why?"

SUE: "I don't know. It must have been so dark I didn't see the other one."

MOM: "Jackie, go outside and play with your whistle. Your father can't read his paper."
JACKIE: "Boy, I'm only eight and I can read it!"

HELEN: "Mom, do you know what I'm going to give you for your birthday?"
MOM: "No, dear, what?"
HELEN: "A nice teapot."
MOM: "But I've got a nice teapot."
HELEN: "No you haven't. I've just dropped it!"

GRANDMA: "Come on, Lucy. I'll give you a penny for a kiss."
LUCY: "I get more than that for taking my castor oil!"

Little girl, having been sent to bring the morning milk in: "Mom, the milkman's been and gone and not come!"

LITTLE SALLY: "Mom, does God go to the bathroom?"
MOM: "No, dear. Why do you ask?"
LITTLE SALLY: "Well, this morning I heard Dad knock on the bathroom door and say, 'Oh, God, are you still in there?'"

*Why do bees hum?*
'Cause they don't know the words.

*How do you make a coat last?*
Make the trousers first.

*Why did a one-handed man cross the road?*
To get to the second-hand shop.

*How do you start a flea race?*
Say "one, two, flea—go!"

*How do you start a teddy-bear race?*
Say, "Ready, teddy—go!"

Two elephants fell over a cliff—boom boom!

*What would you do with a sick wasp?*
  Take it to a waspital.

*Why are ghosts invisible?*
  'Cause they wear see-through clothes.

*What did one witch say to another witch?*
  "Snap, cackle, and pop!"

*Where would you find a prehistoric cow?*
  In a moo-seum.

*Why don't elephants ride bicycles?*
  They haven't got thumbs to ring the bell with.

## From our bookshelf

A Clifftop Tragedy — by Eileen Dover
Moving Day — by Ivor Newhouse
Noisy Nights — by Constance Norah
Drums and Trumpets — by Major Headache
African Pygmies — by R. U. Short
Influenza — by Mike Robe
My Most Embarrassing Moment — by Lucy Lastick
Simple Mathematics — by Algy Brar
The Rifle Range — by Bob Downe
Stranded on the Highway — by Buster Tire
The Return of the Prodigal Son — by Gladys Back

"Why are you crying, sonny?"
   "My brother's lost his school cap."
   "But why should that make *you* cry?"
   "I was wearing it when he lost it."

A boy from a coastal resort had learned to swim in the sea. One day his father took him to a public swimming pool for the first time.

After he had been in the pool for a few minutes, the

boy called his father over and whispered: "Dad, I've swallowed some. Will they mind?"

TONY: "Aw—you're a baby! You're afraid to go upstairs in the dark by yourself!"
TERRY: "I'm not afraid."
TONY: "Yes, you are. 'Fraidy-cat!"
TERRY: "I'm not afraid—you come up with me and see!"

Two brothers had had a fight and were sent to bed without supper. After lying in silence in their beds for ten minutes, the bigger brother wanted to make up, so he whispered, "Pete, are you awake?"

"I'm not telling you," was the sulky reply.

"No, you can't have any more ice cream. It's bad for you to go to bed on a full stomach."

"Oh, Mom . . . I can lie on my side, can't I?"

VISITOR: "You're very quiet, Jennifer."
JENNIFER: "Well, Mom gave me a quarter not to say anything about your red nose."

"Mom, can I have two pieces of cake, please?"

"Certainly—take this piece and cut it in two!"

"Here you are, Uncle, here's some wool from my needle-work classes."

"Thank you, my dear, but what would I want with wool?"

"I don't know, but Dad says you're always wool-gathering."

"Why are you looking at the mirror with your eyes shut?"

"I want to see what I look like when I'm asleep."

"Don't eat the cookies so fast—they'll keep."

"I know, but I want to eat as many as I can before I lose my appetite."

"You youngsters are soft and lazy today. When I was your age I got up at six o'clock every morning and walked five or six miles before breakfast. I used to think nothing of it."

"I don't blame you, Grandpa. I wouldn't think much of it myself."

"Your sister's cooking Sunday lunch for us."
  "Ugh! I suppose that means enthusiasm soup again."
  "Enthusiasm soup? What's that?"
  "She puts everything she's got into it!"

After a visit to the circus, Geoff and Don were discussing the thrills and marvels they had seen.
  "I didn't think much of the knife thrower, did you?" said Geoff.
  "I thought he was super!" enthused Don.
  "Well, I didn't," said Geoff. "He kept chucking those knives at that soppy girl and didn't hit her once!"

"Stuart, you're taking a long time over that letter to Grandma."
  "Well, she can't see very well, Mom, so I'm writing slowly."

"Frankie, have you got your shoes on yet?"
  "Yes, Mom—all except one!"

SISTER: "I've made the chicken soup."
BROTHER: "Thank goodness for that. I thought it was for us!"

MOM: "Mary, how are you getting on with your catechism lessons?"
MARY: "They're very hard, Mom. I wish I could have started with kitty-chism lessons first."

NASTY LITTLE BROTHER: "Hello, Ginger!"
VAIN BIG SISTER: "My hair's not ginger. It's gold."
NASTY LITTLE BROTHER: "Yeah—eighteen *carrot!*"

Little Johnny was playing in the garden and squinting ferociously in the sunlight. His mother came out and said, "Why don't you move out of the sun?"

"Why should I?" demanded Johnny. "I was here first!"

"Mom, you know that vase that's been handed down from generation to generation?"

"Yes."

"Well, this generation's dropped it."

One very stormy night, Mom went upstairs to Little Johnny's bedroom in case he was frightened by all the thunder and lightning.

"Are you all right, Johnny?" she asked softly.

"Yes, Mom," said Johnny. "Is that Dad fooling around with the TV again?"

"My granddad was still alive at the age of a hundred and two!"

"That's nothing. My granddad is still alive at a hundred thirty-three!"

"What? A hundred and thirty-three?"

"Yes—A hundred thirty-three Acacia Avenue!"

Jeremy was showing his sister photographs of his vacation. When they came to one of him sitting on the back of a donkey on the sands, she exclaimed, "Oh, that's nice. But who's that sitting on your back?"

Young Annie asked her big sister for help with her arithmetic homework.

"Oh, no," said big sister primly, "it wouldn't be right."

"I know that," said Annie, "but at least you could *try*, Sis!"

A little girl was being driven very erratically in a car by her grandma. "Don't go around corners so fast, Gran," she pleaded.

"Do as I do, dear," said the sweet old lady, "and close your eyes!"

"My big sister can play the piano by ear."

"That's nothing. My big brother can fiddle with his whiskers!"

Trevor came rushing in to his dad.

"Dad," he puffed, "is it true that an apple a day keeps the doctor away?"

"That's what they say," said his dad.

"Well, give me an apple—quick. I've just broken the doctor's window!"

A woman with a baby in her arms was sitting in the waiting room at a railway station, sobbing bitterly. Up came a porter and asked her what the trouble was.

"Oh, dear me," she cried, "some people were in here, and they were so rude to me about my son! I'm all upset—they said he was so ugly."

"There, there," said the porter soothingly. "Don't worry

about it. I tell you what—how about a nice cup of tea?"

"You're very kind," she said, wiping her eyes, "that would be very nice."

"And while I'm at it," he said, "how about a banana for your monkey?"

LITTLE GIRL: "Mommy, why do you feed baby brother with a spoon?"
MOMMY: "Because he's still learning to eat."
LITTLE GIRL: "Then why not give him a learner's plate?"

LEN: "Do you know, my dad's a magician."
TOM: "Is he really?"
LEN: "Yeah. One wave of his magic slipper and I disappear!"

A schoolboy went home with a pain in his stomach. "Well, sit down and drink your tea," said his mother. "Your stomach hurts because it's empty. It'll be all right when you've got something in it."

Shortly afterward Dad came home from the office, complaining of a headache.

"That's because it's empty," said his bright son. "You'd be all right if you had something in it."

"How did you get on with your arithmetic exam?"

"I only got one sum wrong."

"That's very good. How many were there?"

"Twelve."

"Twelve! So you got eleven of the sums right?"

"No—they were the ones I couldn't do!"

MOM: "Jimmy, where are you off to now?"

JIMMY: "I'm going to join the army."

MOM: "But legally you're only an infant."

JIMMY: "That's all right. I'm going to join the infantry."

Teddy came thundering down the stairs, much to his father's annoyance.

"Teddy," he called, "how many more times do I have to tell you to come down those stairs quietly! Now, go back upstairs and come down like a civilized human being."

There was a silence, and Teddy reappeared in the front room.

"That's better," said his father. "Now in the future will you always come down the stairs like that."

"Suits me," said Teddy. "I slid down the bannister."

LUKE: "Mom, am I made of sage and parsley and breadcrumbs?"

MOM: "Of course not. Why do you ask?"
LUKE: "Because that big boy from the corner said he's going to knock the stuffing out of me tomorrow."

The Jones family was just about to leave on their annual vacation. "Have you packed everything?" Mrs. Jones asked her small son.

"Yes, Mom," he answered.

"Are you sure?" she said suspiciously. "Have you packed your soap?"

"Soap?" he said in dismay. "I thought this was supposed to be a vacation!"

Young Harry came home bruised and battered and with his clothes all torn. His father decided to use tact rather than force on this occasion, and said to him: "Harry, why is it that you're always fighting? In this life you must learn to give and take."

"But I did, Dad," said Harry. "He took my caramel apple, so I gave him a thump on the nose."

*What did the necklace say to the hat?*
You go on ahead—I'll hang around.

*Who gets the sack as soon as he starts work?*
   A postman.

*What has twenty-two legs, two wings, and is yellow all over?*
   A Chinese soccer team...

*Why did the apple turnover?*
   Because it saw the jam roll.

If a prehistoric monster took an exam, he'd pass with extinction.

*What do cornflakes wear on their feet?*
   K-logs [clogs].

*What goes zzub-zzub?*
   A bee flying backward.

*Why was the ghost arrested?*
   Because he hadn't got a haunting license.

*On what side of a school should an elm tree grow?*
    On the outside.

*Why did the schoolboy throw a clock out the window?*
    To see time fly.

## *From our bookshelf*

| | |
|---|---|
| The Naughty Farm Boy | *by* Enid Spankin |
| The Unknown Author | *by* Ann Onymous |
| The Postscript | *by* Adeline Extra |
| Jungle Fever | *by* Amos Quito |
| Tea for Two | *by* Roland Butta |
| The Long Hot Summer | *by* I. Scream |
| Try and Try Again | *by* Percy Vere |
| It Pays to Advertise | *by* Bill Sticker |
| The Barber of Seville | *by* Ray Zerr |
| The Drawing Lesson | *by* Art Master |

"My brother's one of the biggest stick-up men in town."
    "Gosh, is he really?"
    "Yes, he's a six-foot-six bill-poster."

Nutty Aunt Muriel received a letter one morning, and upon reading it burst into floods of tears.

"What's the matter?" asked her companion.

"Oh, dear," sobbed Auntie, "it's my favorite nephew. He has three feet."

"Three feet?" exclaimed her friend. "Surely that's not possible."

"Well," said Auntie, "his mother's just written to tell me he's grown another foot!"

Little Susie was staying with her grandmother in the country for a few days.

"Would you like to see the cuckoo come out of the cuckoo clock?" asked her grandmother.

"I'd rather see Grandpa come out of the grandfather clock," said Susie.

GRANDPA: "Why are you crying, Robin?"

ROBIN: "'Cause Dad won't play Cowboys and Indians with me."

GRANDPA: "Never mind, I'll play Cowboys and Indians with you."

ROBIN: "That's no good—you've been scalped already."

Two boys were boasting about their respective dads.

"My dad's got so many gold teeth he has to sleep with

his head in a safe," said one.

"That's nothing," said the other. "My dad rides around all day with his pockets full of money."

"What does he do?"

"He's a bus conductor."

A naughty boy was caught up a tree stealing apples. "Come down this minute!" shouted the furious owner. "Or I'll tell your father!"

"You can tell him now," replied the boy. "He's up here with me."

Big sister had been taking singing lessons and was demonstrating her vocal prowess to her unenthusiastic little brother.

"What would you like me to sing for you next?" she asked brightly.

"Do you know 'Loch Lomond'?" he asked.

"Yes," she replied.

"Well, go and jump in it!"

Dad was in a terrible temper over his son's latest school report.

"It says here that you came last in a class of twenty," he raged. "That's dreadful!"

"It might be worse, Dad," said the unrepentant boy. "There might have been more kids in the class!"

Dad was asking Brenda how she had coped with her exams. "Did you have any problems with the questions?" he asked.

"Oh, no difficulty with the questions, Dad," said Brenda. "It was the answers that bothered me."

SISTER: "You're stupid! You don't know nothing!"
BROTHER: "Oh, yes I do! It's what Dad gave me for weeding the garden last Saturday."

A small boy was watching his big sister carefully making up before going out to a dance.

"I dunno why you bother, Sis," he said. "You're so ugly."

"How dare you!" she said, furious. "I'll have you know I have plenty of men at my feet!"

"Yeah," he drawled. "Foot doctors!"

"My dad bought my mom a mink outfit for her birthday."

"Wow, did he?"

"Yeah. Two steel traps and a shotgun."

"My uncle Ben and aunt Flo haven't had a fight for five years."

"That's wonderful."

"Not really. Uncle Ben lives in China."

BIG SISTER: "Here, Johnny, try one of my cakes."

SMALL BROTHER (biting into one): "Ugh! It's horrible!"

BIG SISTER: "The trouble with you is you've no taste. It distinctly says in my cookbook that this recipe is delicious."

"Nick, what's your big brother doing now that he's left school?"

"He's taking French, German, and Italian."

"Gosh! That must take a lot of studying."

"No—he's an elevator operator in the Hotel International."

BIG SISTER: "Try some of my sponge cake."

BROTHER (nibbling on a piece): "It's a bit tough, Sis."

BIG SISTER: "Yes, I can't understand it. I bought a fresh sponge from the store specially."

GRANDMA: "I'll take your baby brother for a walk in his stroller, shall I?"

LITTLE GIRL: "That's not much of a walk, Grandma."

"How did your mother know you hadn't washed your face?"

"I forgot to wet the soap."

TASMIN: "Mom, can I play the piano?"

MOM: "Not till you've washed your hands. They're filthy."

TASMIN: "Oh, Mom—I'll only play on the black notes."

MOM: "I thought you were going to see your dentist this afternoon."

DAD: "That's right."

MOM: "Then how is it that when I was on the bus going to do my shopping I saw you going into the football game with a short, fat man?"

DAD: "That's my dentist!"

SUSIE: "My baby brother's only a year old and he's been walking for six months!"

ANNIE: "Really? He must be very tired."

"Are you writing a thank-you letter to Grandpa like I told you?"

"Yes, Mom."

"Your handwriting seems very large."

"Well, Grandpa's deaf, so I'm writing very loud."

"You're very late in coming from school, aren't you?"

"I stayed in for fencing lessons, Dad."

"Right—tomorrow you can help me mend the one behind the garage."

Joey Brown was having afternoon tea with his Grandma. "Would you like some bread and butter, Joey?" she asked.

"Yes, thank you, Grandma," he said.

"That's a good boy," said Grandma. "I like to hear you saying 'thank you.'"

"If you want to hear me say it again," added Joey, "you can put some jam on it!"

"Mom, I caught a trout two feet long!"

"Did you? Where is it?"

"Well, I remembered our frying pan is only about nine inches across, so I threw it back!"

"Come on, Charles, I'll take you to the zoo."

"If the zoo wants me, let 'em come and get me!"

"Oh, you're such a pest on vacation. I'll be glad when you're back at school!"

"I'll be there longer this term, Mom."

"Why, has term time been extended?"
"No, but I'll be taller, won't I?"

"Dad, what are all those holes in the new garden shed?"
"They're knotholes."
"What do you mean 'they're not holes'? I can put my finger into them."

KINDLY OLD LADY: "I suppose your new baby sister is a lovely pink and white?"
NASTY CHILD: "No, she's a horrible yeller."

"Eat your dinner."
"I'm waiting for the mustard to cool off."

"You've got your socks on inside out."
"I know, Mom, but there are holes on the other side."

"Dad, is an ox a sort of a male cow?"
"Sort of, yes."
"And 'equine' means something to do with horses, doesn't it?"
"That's right."
"So what's an equinox?"

"Grandpa, can you make a noise like a frog?"
"I don't think I've ever tried, me lad. Why?"

"'Cause Dad says we'll get ten thousand dollars when you croak."

At the seaside, Mom waxed lyrical at the beauty of the sunset over the sea.

"Doesn't the sun look wonderful setting on the horizon?" she breathed.

"Yes," said young Sammy, "and there won't even be a hiss when it touches the water!"

A distraught mother rushed into the backyard, where eight-year-old Tommy was banging on the bottom of an old upturned bucket with a poker.

"What *do* you think you're playing?" she demanded.

"I'm just entertaining the baby," explained Tommy.

"Where is the baby?" asked his mom.

"Under the bucket."

Dad was furious about Sonny's school report. "I've never read anything like it!" he roared. "It says here that you're nothing but a little terror! What does this mean?"

"It means, Dad," said the object of the report, "that I'm the son of a big terror."

"Geoffrey, pick up your feet when you walk!"
"Why, Mom? I only have to put them down again."

"My brother's in the hospital."
"What's wrong with him?"
"He's got spotted fever."
"Oh, boy! Is it serious?"
"No—it was spotted in time."

*When is it bad luck to have a black cat follow you?*
When you're a mouse.

*Ten cats were in a boat and one jumped out. How many were left?*
None, because the others were copycats.

*What's brown and can see just as well from either end?*
A horse with its eyes shut.

*If a red house is made of red bricks and a yellow house is made of yellow bricks, what is a greenhouse made of?*
Glass...

*What animals need oiling?*
   Mice, because they squeak.

*How do you stop a dog from barking in the back seat of a car?*
   Put him in the front seat.

*What is it that's got meat in it, also bread and tomatoes, an orange, is tied up in plastic, and flies through belfries?*
   The Lunchpack of Notre Dame.

*What is it that goes 99 plonk?*
   A centipede with a wooden leg.

*What is it that goes 999 plonk?*
   A millipede with a wooden leg.

*What did one centipede say to the other centipede as they watched a lady centipede walk past?*
   "There goes a lovely pair of legs, pair of legs, pair of legs, pair of legs. . . ."

MOM: "Maria, was that the stepladder I heard falling over?"
MARIA: "Yes, Mom."
MOM: "Has your dad fallen down?"
MARIA: "No, mom, he's still hanging on the curtain rod!"

A small boy had the misfortune to have the cheapest dad in the world. One rainy day, the little lad came in shivering with the wet and the cold and said, "Dad, my boots let the water in."

"So what?" said his flinty-hearted parent. "They let it out again, don't they?"

A little girl from a very poor family went into the local baker's shop. "My mom wants a large loaf, please," she said, putting down her pennies. "And would you please cut it in slices with a jammy knife?"

"Is this your brother?"
  "Yes, vicar."
  "He's very small, isn't he?"
  "Well, he's only my half-brother."

"Dad, I don't want to go to Australia!"
  "Shut up and keep digging."

A nine-year-old was digging in the garden when his mom came out and asked him what he was doing.

"I'm collecting slugs, Mom," was the happy answer.

"Oh," said his mom unenthusiastically. "And what are you going to do with them?"

"Press them!"

MOM: "Horace, why are you crying?"
HORACE: "I've hurt my finger, Mom."
MOM: "When did you do that?"
HORACE: "Half an hour ago."
MOM: "I didn't hear you crying then."
HORACE: "No, I thought you were out."

"Mervyn, your great-grandfather is one hundred years old today! Isn't that wonderful?"

"Huh! It's taken him long enough to do it."

"My dad's a sorter in the White House."

"What sort of sorter?"

"A sorter window cleaner."

"Giles, we're having very important guests for lunch today, so clean yourself up and make yourself presentable, please."

"Why—they're not going to eat me, are they?"

"Now then, Deidre, eat up all your greens like a good girl. They're good for the complexion, you know."

"But I don't want to have a green complexion!"

A child one Christmas asked for some paper and crayons in order to draw a crib. Eventually the artistic masterpiece was displayed for parental approval. The manger, the shepherds, Jesus, and the Holy Family were duly admired.

"But what's that in the corner?" asked Mother.

"Oh, that's their TV," replied the tot.

"That was kind of you to let your sister have first go with your skates."

"I'm waiting to see if the ice is thick enough."

MOM: "How was your first day at school?"

JOHNNY: "It was all right, except for some guy called Sir who kept spoiling the fun."

"What did you learn in school today, son?"

"I learned that those sums you did for me were wrong!"

"Rebecca, it's taking you a long time to put salt in the salt shaker."

"Well, Mom, you can't get much at a time through that little hole in the top."

MOM: "Come on, Mike. Time waits for no man, you know."

MIKE: "Yes it does, Mom."

MOM: "What do you mean?"

MIKE: "Well, when Dad and I were walking back from church last Sunday and we passed the bar on the corner, he said to me: 'Wait here—I'll just stop a few minutes.'"

"What would you like?"

"Cake."

"Cake what?"

"Cake first."

"Jimmy, what did I say I'd do if I caught you smoking cigarettes again?"

"That's funny, Dad—I can't remember, either."

"Julia, this report is most disappointing. I promised you a bicycle if you passed your exams. What have you been doing with yourself?"

"Learning to ride a bike."

"Do you look in the mirror after you've washed?"

"No, I look in the towel!"

"Dad, I bet there's something I can do that you can't do."

"What's that, son?"

"Grow up!"

DAD: "Gary, how was your first day at school?"

GARY: "Okay, Dad, but I didn't get my present yet."

DAD: "What present is that?"

GARY: "Well, the teacher said to me, 'Gary, sit there for the present.' Maybe I'll get it tomorrow."

GRANDMA: "You've left all your crusts, Mary. When I was your age I ate every one."

MARY: "Do you still like crusts, Grandma?"

GRANDMA: "Yes, I do."

MARY: "Well, you can have mine."

Benjamin, go and kiss your auntie good-bye."

"Why, I didn't do anything!"

"Will you have some pudding to finish up with?"

"No, I'll have another bun to go on with!"

Pa was taking Danny around the museum where they came across a magnificent stuffed lion in a glass case.

"Pa," asked the puzzled Danny, "how did they shoot the lion without breaking the glass?"

"How did your exams go?"

"I nearly got a hundred in every subject."

"How do you mean—nearly a hundred?"

"Well, I got the zeros."

"Dad, a man came by while you were out."

"Did he have a bill?"

"No, just an ordinary nose like everyone else."

146

*What note do you get if an elephant playing the piano falls down a mine shaft?*
A Flat miner [A flat minor].

*Why is a banana skin like a pullover?*
Because it's easy to slip on.

*Why is a lazy dog like a hill?*
Because it's a slow pup [slope up].

*Why do we go to bed?*
Because the bed won't come to us.

*What does an elephant do when it rains?*
Gets wet.

*Who drives all his customers away?*
A taxi driver.

*Why is a guidebook like a pair of handcuffs?*
Because it is for tourists [two wrists].

*"If a fellow met a fibber in a fallow field"*—how many f's in that?

None—there are no f's in "that."

What can you give someone and still keep?

Your word.

*Have you heard the story of the church bell?*

It hasn't ever been tolled [told].

An aunt who very rarely came visiting was very touched by the attention paid to her by the son of the house.

"You've been very nice to me this afternoon, Johnny," she said. "I do believe that you don't want me to go."

"You're right—I don't, Auntie. Dad says he's going to give me a good hiding as soon as you've gone."

"Come here, you greedy wretch. I'll teach you to eat all your sister's birthday candy."

"It's all right, Dad. I know how."

MOM: "Nicholas, don't be mean. Let your little brother play with your marbles if he wants to."

NICHOLAS: "Oh, Mom! He wants to keep them."

MOM: "I'm sure he doesn't."

NICHOLAS: "Well, he's swallowed two already!"

MOM: "Susan, just look at the mess you're in! What *have* you been doing?"

SUSAN: "I fell in a puddle, Mom."

MOM: "In your new dress?"

SUSAN: "Well, I didn't have time to change."

DAD (to daughter): "Well, Anne, I suppose that boyfriend of yours will be coming around after supper?"

SMALL BROTHER: "That's all he *does* come around for!"

"I had a funny dream last night, Mom."

"Did you?"

"I dreamed I was awake, but when I woke up I found I was asleep!"

PRUNELLA: "Mom, Simon broke my doll."

MOM: "How did he do that?"

PRUNELLA: "I hit him on the head with it."

"Why are your class marks always so low?"

"Because I sit in the last desk at the back, Dad."

"What difference does that make?"

"Well, there are so many of us in the class that when it's my turn for marks there aren't many left."

"What's your father's walk in life?"

"He's a bit bowlegged—why?"

"Mom, how do you spell 'high'?"

"H-I-G-H. Why, what is your composition about?"

"High-enas."

"My dad hasn't done a day's work since 1968."

"Why not?"

"He's a night watchman."

"Mom, do you think the baby would like some blotting paper to eat?"

"No, dear, I don't think he would. Why?"
"He's just swallowed a bottle of ink."

"Barbara, what are you doing out there in the rain?"
"Getting wet!"

"Vicar told us that in the Bible it says we're made of dust."
"That's right."
"So when I go swimming, why don't I get muddy?"

DAD: "Boy, I slept like a log last night."
KEN: "I know you did, Dad. I heard you sawing it."

"Jeremy, I want you to wash before your music teacher arrives."
"I have, Mom."
"Did you wash your ears?"
"Well . . . I washed the one that'll be next to her."

"Dad, if I plant this seed in the garden, will it grow into an orange tree?"

"It might, son, yes."

"That's funny—it's a lemon seed."

"What happened to all those mince pies? I told you you couldn't have one, and now there's only one left."

"That's the one I haven't had, Mom."

Paul's teacher had had enough of his pranks and impertinence in the schoolroom, so he wrote a letter of complaint to Paul's father.

"Paul," roared Dad, "come here! What's all this about? Your teacher says he finds it impossible to teach you anything!"

"I told you he was no good," said Paul.

"Now, little man, what are you going to give your sister for Christmas?"

"Well, last Christmas I gave her measles."

Jimmy was caught by his mother in the pantry. "And what do you think you're up to?" she asked furiously.

"I'm up to my seventh jam tart," said Jimmy, "but they're only little ones, Mom!"

"Dad, the boy next door said I look just like you."

"Did he now? And what did you say?"

"Nothing. He's bigger than me."

A scoutmaster asked one of his troop what good deed he had done for the day.

"Well, Skip," said the scout, "Mom only had one dose of castor oil left, so I let my baby brother have it."

Yet another bad school report was received by an irate father.

"Stevie, I'm not at all pleased with your report this term," he said furiously.

"I told the teacher you wouldn't be," said Stevie, "but he insisted on sending it just the same."

"Mom, will you wash my face?"

"Why can't you wash it yourself?"

"'Cause that'll mean getting my hands wet, and they don't need washing!"

"So you are distantly related to the family next door, are you?"

"Yes—their dog is our dog's brother."

A rather stern aunt had been staying with Sharon's parents, and one day she said to the little girl, "Well, Sharon, I'm going tomorrow. Are you sorry?"

"Oh, yes, Auntie," replied Sharon. "I thought you were going today."

"No, Billy, you can't play with the hammer. You'll hurt your fingers."

"No I won't, Dad. Sis is going to hold the nails for me."

"Joyce, how many more times must I tell you to come away from that cake plate?"

"No more, Mom. It's empty!"

"Eve, do you know a girl called Clare Cook?"

"Yes, Mom. She sleeps next to me in geography class."

"Dad, are caterpillars good to eat?"

"No, son. Why?"

"'Cause you've just eaten one on your lettuce."

"Tell me, Jason, do you like going to school?"

"Yes, Uncle Harry, I like *going* to school—it's when I get there that I don't enjoy myself much."

"Mom, if someone broke your best vase, what would you do?"

"I'd spank him and send him to bed without any supper!"

"Well, you'd better get the strap. Dad just broke it!"

A visitor to Geoffrey's house remarked at lunch on the friendliness of Geoff's dog.

"He's wagging his tail at me and sitting up all the time!" said the visitor, pleased.

"I'm not surprised," said Geoffrey. "You're eating off his plate."

"You've been fighting again—you've lost two of your front teeth!"

"I haven't lost them, Mom. I have 'em in my pocket."

"Ma, Ma! Dad's fallen over the cliff!"

"My goodness! Is he hurt?"

"I dunno—he hadn't stopped falling when I left!"

Midge was scribbling industriously over some paper with a pencil when her mother asked what she was drawing.

"I'm not drawing, Mom," she said indignantly. "I'm writing a letter to Jenny."

"But you can't write," Mom pointed out.

"That's all right," said Midge. "Jenny can't read."

"Dad, would you like to save some money?"

"I certainly would, son. Any suggestions?"

"Sure. Why not buy me a bike, then I won't wear my shoes out so fast."

"Mom, the vicar says that we're made out of dust and unto dust we shall return."

"That's right, Ben."

"Well, you'd better look under my bed, 'cause there's someone there either coming or going."

"Who broke the window?"

"It was Andrew, Dad. He ducked when I threw a stone at him."

GRANDMA: "Sylvester, I wouldn't slide down the banister like that if I were you."

SYLVESTER: "Why, how would you slide down them, then, Grandma?"

# Waiter . . . !

—there's a flea in my soup.
  I'll tell him to hop it.

—what's this fly doing in my soup?
  Looks like the breast stroke to me, sir.

—my plate's wet.
  That's not wet, sir—that's the soup!

—what do you call this?
  That's bean soup, sir.
  I don't care what it's been—what is it now?

157

—send the chef here. I wish to complain about this disgusting meal.

I'm afraid you'll have to wait, sir. He just went out for his dinner.

—I'll have the pie, please.

Anything with it, sir?

If it's anything like last time, I'd better have a hammer and chisel.

—do you call this a three-course meal?

That's right, sir. Two French fries and a pea.

—I'll have my bill now.

How did you find your steak, sir?

Oh, I just moved the potato and there it was.

—this soup tastes funny.

So why don't you laugh?

—what do you call this?

Cottage pie, sir.

Well, I've just bitten on a piece of the door.

—there's a dead fly in my soup.
   What do you expect for a dime—a live one?

—there's a bird in my soup.
   That's all right, sir. It's bird's-nest soup.

—there's a dead beetle in my soup.
   Yes, sir, they're not very good swimmers.

—there's a fly in my soup!
   Well, keep quiet about it, or everyone will want one.

—bring me a fried egg with finger marks in it, some
lukewarm greasy French fries, and a portion of watery
cabbage.
   We don't do food like that, sir!
   You did yesterday.

—this coffee tastes like mud!
   I'm not surprised, sir. It was ground only a few minutes
ago.

—your tie is in my soup!

That's all right, sir. It's not shrinkable.

—your thumb's in my soup!

That's all right, sir. It's not hot.

—what's this in my soup?

I dunno, sir. I can't tell one bug from another.

—do you serve crabs?

Sit down, sir—we serve anybody.

—have you got frogs' legs?

Certainly, sir.

Then hop into the kitchen and get me a steak!

—does the pianist play requests?

Yes, sir.

Then ask him to play tiddlywinks till I've finished my meal.

—my bill, please.

How did you find your luncheon, sir?

With a magnifying glass.

—have you got asparagus?
We don't serve sparrers, and my name's not Gus!

—this lobster's only got one claw.
I guess he's been in a fight, sir.
Well, bring me the winner!

—why have you given me my dinner in a feedbag?
The headwaiter says you eat like a horse.

—there's a dead fly in my soup!
Yes, sir, it's the hot water that kills 'em.

—there's a twig in my soup.
Yes, sir, we've got branches everywhere.

—I can't eat this!
Why not, sir?
You haven't given me a knife and fork.

—my knife is blunt and my steak is like leather.
I would strop the knife on the steak then, sir.

—if this is flounder, then I'm an idiot.

You're right, sir—it *is* flounder.

—I think I'd like a little game.

Checkers or tiddleywinks, sir?

—is this all you've got to eat?

No, sir, I'll be having a nice shepherd's pie when I get home.

—how long have you been here?

Six months, sir.

Ah, then, it can't be you who took my order.

—there's a fly in my butter.

No there isn't.

I tell you there's a fly in my butter!

And I tell you there isn't. It isn't a fly; it's a moth. And it isn't butter; it's margarine. So there!

—I'll have soup and fish.

I'd have the fish first if I were you, sir. It's just about to spoil.

—you're not fit to serve a pig!
I'm doing my best, sir.

—bring me tea without milk.
We don't have any milk, sir. How about tea without cream?

—I'll pay my bill now.
This dollar's bad, sir.
So was the meal.

—how long will my sausages be?
Oh, about three or four inches if you're lucky.

—bring me a glass of milk and a Dover sole.
Fillet?
Yes, to the brim.

—this egg tastes rather strong.
Never mind, sir, the tea's nice and weak.

—I'll have a chop; no—make that a steak.
I'm a waiter, sir; not a magician!

—I asked for bread with my dinner.
  It's in the sausages, sir.

—where is my honey?
  She left last week, sir.

—there's a hair in my honey.
  It must have dropped off the comb, sir!

—that dog just ran off with my roast lamb!
  Yes, it's very popular, sir.

—this bread's got sand in it.
  That's to stop the butter slipping off, sir.

—there's a button in my soup.
  Oh, thank you, sir. I've been looking for that everywhere.

—there's no chicken in this chicken pie.
  So what? You don't get dog in a dog biscuit, do you?

—there's a worm on my plate.
  That's your sausage, sir.

—there's a fly in my soup.
  That's all right, sir. He won't drink much.

—there's a fly swimming in my soup.
  So what do you expect me to do—call a lifeguard?

—what's the meaning of this fly in my teacup?
  I wouldn't know, sir. I'm a waiter, not a fortune teller.

—this coffee tastes like soap.
  Then that must be tea, sir—the coffee tastes like glue.

—in the future I'd like my soup without.
  Without what, sir?
  Without your thumb in it!

—is this a lamb chop or a pork chop?
  Can't you tell by the taste?
  No, I can't.
  Then what does it matter?

—there's a beetle in my soup; send the manager here.
  That won't do any good—he's frightened of 'em as well!

# The Happiest Days of Your life

## and other fairy tales

TEACHER: "Who can tell me something of importance that didn't exist one hundred years ago?"
SMALLEST GIRL IN THE CLASS: "Me!"

TEACHER: "Where are you from, Andy?"
ANDY: "Scotland, miss."
TEACHER: "What part?"
ANDY: "All of me, miss."

TEACHER: "What is an Indian's wife called?"
A GIRL: "A squaw, miss."
TEACHER: "Quite right. And what are Indian babies called?"
A BOY: "Squawkers?"

TEACHER: "Tommy Russell, you're late again."
TOMMY: "Sorry, sir. It's my bus—it's always coming late."
TEACHER: "Well, if it's late again tomorrow, catch an earlier one."

TEACHER: "Alan, give me a sentence starting with I."
ALAN: "I is—"
TEACHER: "No, Alan. You must always say 'I *am*.'"
ALAN: "Oh, right. 'I am the ninth letter of the alphabet.'"

Latin's a dead language,
As dead as dead can be;
It killed off all the Romans,
And now it's killing me.

*The author's Latin master was nicknamed "Charlie," giving rise to the following:*

Charlibus sittibus
On the deskinorum.
Deskibus collapsibus.
Charlie on the floorum.

TEACHER: "Albert, who were the Phoenicians?"
ALBERT: "The people who invented Phoenician [Venetian] blinds."

When one teacher told his class to write the longest sentence they could compose, a bright spark wrote: "Imprisonment for Life"!

Jeremy was sprawling half out of his desk and chewing gum in a very slovenly manner, causing his teacher to say, "Jeremy—take that gum out of your mouth and put your feet in!"

TEACHER: "Why is it said that lightning never strikes the same place twice?"
ROY: "Because after it's struck once, the same place isn't there anymore!"

TEACHER: "Why was the period between AD 500 and AD 4200 known as the Dark Ages?"
HEATHER: "Because those were the days of the (k)nights."

MOM: "Hello, Jack. Learn anything new in school today?"
JACK: "Yeah, how to get out of class by stuffing red ink up my nose."

TEACHER: "Ivor, where is Felixstowe?"
IVOR: "On the end of Felix foot!"

TEACHER: "What is love, Derek?"
DEREK: "Well, I *like* my mom and dad, but I *love* bubble gum."

TEACHER: "Jill, what do you know about Good Friday?"
JILL: "He did the housework for Robinson Crusoe."

TEACHER: "Fiona, give me a sentence containing the word 'gruesome.'"
FIONA: "Er—er—my dad didn't shave for a week and grew some whiskers."

VICAR: "To do anything in life you must start at the bottom and work up."
SMALL CHOIRBOY: "What about swimming, Vicar?"

TEACHER: "Spell the word 'needle,' Kenneth."
KENNETH: "N-e-i-"
TEACHER: "No, Kenneth, there's no 'i' in needle."
KENNETH: "Then it's a rotten needle!"

The school inspector asked the class to tell him a number. "Twenty-seven," called out one pupil, and the inspector wrote down 72 on the blackboard. No one said anything, so again he asked the class for a number. "Twenty-four," came a voice, and again the inspector wrote on the blackboard—42. And again no one said a word. "Can I have another number, please?" asked the inspector. "Thirty-three," shouted someone, and a quiet voice at the back added, "Let's see him fool around with that one!"

TEACHER: "Carol, what is 'can't' short for?"
CAROL: "Cannot."
TEACHER: "And what is 'don't' short for?"
CAROL: "Doughnut!"

*If sixteen boys share a chocolate cake, what is the time?*
    A quarter to four.

*What is a sailor who is married with seven children called?*
    Daddy.

*Why did the chicken cross the road?*
  For fowl [foul] purposes.

*When would you be glad to be down and out?*
  After a bumpy plane trip.

*What did the toothpaste say to the brush?*
  Give me a squeeze and I'll meet you outside the tube.

*What's strange about carpets?*
  They're bought by the yard and worn by the foot.

*What holds water yet is full of holes?*
  A sponge.

*Where do flies go in wintertime?*
  To the glassworks to be turned into bluebottles.

*Why did the snow-drop?*
  'Cause it heard the cro-cuss!

TEACHER: "Ford, you're late for school again. What is it this time?"

FORD: "I sprained my ankle, sir."

TEACHER: "That's a lame excuse."

TEACHER: "Williams, your writing has improved."

WILLIAMS: "Thank you, sir."

TEACHER: "Now I've discovered what an atrocious speller you are!"

TEACHER: "Smith, now that you've kindly consented to come to school, what would you like to do?"

SMITH: "Go home."

TEACHER: "Jane, what's five and three?"

JANE: "Don't know, miss."

TEACHER: "You silly girl—it's eight, of course."

JANE: "But yesterday you said that four and four was eight!"

TEACHER: "Ralph, what are two and two?"

RALPH: "Four."

TEACHER: "That's good."

RALPH: "Good? It's perfect!"

A stern school inspector was putting one class through their paces.

"You, boy," he roared, pointing at one nervous child. "Who signed Magna Carta?"

"Please, sir, it wasn't me!" came the agonized answer.

A little girl was playing in the park when a kindly old lady started talking to her.

"And do you go to school?" she asked.

"No," was the sulky answer, "I'm sent!"

Two friends were talking at recess.

"Would you like to hear a poem?" asked one.

"Okay—as long as it rhymes," said the other. "I only like poetry if it rhymes."

"Oh, you'll like this one. Here goes:

    'A silly little girl whose name was Nellie,
    Fell into the water right up to her knees.'

"But that didn't rhyme," came the complaint.

"No," said the poet. "The water wasn't deep enough."

TEACHER: "How old would a person be who was born in 1935?"

PUPIL: "Er . . . er . . . man or woman?"

A truant officer caught a boy up a tree in the park during school time.

"When are you coming down?" he called.

"When you go away!" was the saucy answer.

TEACHER: "Jones, you should have been in the classroom at nine o'clock."

JONES: "Why—did I miss something good?"

TEACHER: "Martha, what does the word 'trickle' mean?"

MARTHA: "To run slowly."

TEACHER: "Quite right. And what does the word 'anecdote' mean?"

MARTHA: "A short, funny tale."

TEACHER: "Right again. Now, can you give me a sentence with both of those words in it?"

MARTHA: "Er—our dog trickled down the street wagging his anecdote!"

TEACHER: "What is the plural of mouse?"

STUDENT: "Mice."

TEACHER: "And what is the plural of baby?"

STUDENT: "Twins."

TEACHER: "Find Australia on the map for me, Johnny."

JOHNNY: "It's there, sir."

TEACHER: "That's right. Now, Sammy, who discovered Australia?"

SAMMY: "Johnny, sir."

TEACHER: "Now, Harrison, if your father borrows ten dollars from me and pays me back at a dollar a month, at the end of six months how much will he owe me?"

HARRISON: "Ten dollars."

TEACHER: "I'm afraid you don't know much about arithmetic, Harrison."

HARRISON: "I'm afraid you don't know much about my father, sir."

TEACHER: "Now, Jonathan, if I gave you three rabbits and then the next day I gave you five rabbits, how many rabbits would you have?"

JONATHAN: "Nine, sir."

TEACHER: "Nine?"

JONATHAN: "I've got one already, sir."

TEACHER: "Why are you standing on your head, Jackson?"

JACKSON: "Just turning things over in my mind, sir."

TEACHER: "Martin, I've taught you everything I know, and you're *still* ignorant!"

Anthony Brown had been fooling around in class, so his teacher told him to stay in and write out a sentence containing no fewer than fifty words. Tony thought for a few minutes and then submitted the following sentence, after which he was allowed to go home—for his ingenuity as much as for his skill at composition!

This was his sentence:

"Mrs. Smith wanted to call her cat in for the night, so she went to the front door, opened it, and called: 'Here, kitty, kitty, kitty, kitty, kitty, kitty, kitty, kitty, kitty, kitty, kitty, kitty, kitty, kitty, kitty, kitty, kitty, kitty, kitty, kitty, kitty, kitty, kitty, kitty, kitty, kitty, kitty!'"

TEACHER: "Charles, what did Sir Walter Raleigh say as he dropped his cloak before Queen Elizabeth the First?"
CHARLES: "Step on it, kid!"

TEACHER (to unruly class): "Now this afternoon I want to tell you about a hippopotamus. Please pay attention, all of you! If you don't look at me you'll never know what a hippopotamus is like!"

TEACHER: "Today I'm going to instruct you on Mount Everest."

JOHNNY: "Will we be back in time for 'Sesame Street,' sir?"

TEACHER: "Shirley, what is the Dog Star?"

SHIRLEY: "Rin-Tin-Tin, miss."

TEACHER: "Victor, if I say 'I have went,' that is wrong, isn't it?"

VICTOR: "Yes, sir, 'cause you *ain't* went—you're still here!"

TEACHER: "Alexandra, will you correct the following sentence, please: 'the bull and the cow is in the field.'"

ALEXANDRA: "That should be 'the cow and the bull is in the field,' miss. Ladies should always go before gentlemen."

TEACHER: "Daphne, name the four seasons."

DAPHNE: "Salt, mustard, pepper, and vinegar."

NATHAN: "Hey, George—I'm leaving school on Friday!"

GEORGE: "Are you? Why?"

NATHAN: "To have my tea."

TEACHER: "Doris, what's the opposite of misery?"
DORIS: "Happiness."
TEACHER: "Correct. And what's the opposite of sadness?"
DORIS: "Gladness."
TEACHER: "Correct. And the opposite of woe?"
DORIS: "Giddyap!"

*Why are tall people lazier than short people?*
Because they're longer in bed.

*How do you make a pipe lighter?*
Take the tobacco out.

*Why is a cat on the seashore like Christmas?*
Because both have sandy claws [Santa Claus].

*How can you communicate with a fish?*
Drop him a line.

*What do ghosts eat for breakfast?*
Dreaded wheat.

*Do you know what Zulus do with banana skins?*
   Throw them away, of course...

*Why do we call money "bread"?*
   'Cause everybody "kneads" it.

*Why do businessmen carry umbrellas?*
   'Cause umbrellas can't walk.

*What is the hottest letter of the alphabet?*
   B, because it makes oil boil.

## From our bookshelf

| | |
|---|---|
| Swimming the Channel | *by* Frances Near |
| At the North Pole | *by* I. C. Blast |
| At the South Pole | *by* Ann Tarctic |
| The Bullfighter | *by* Matt Adore |
| The Farmer's Wife | *by* Mike Howe |
| The Tiger's Revenge | *by* Claud Body |
| Rice Growing | *by* Paddy Field |
| Aches and Pains | *by* Arthur Ritis |

The arithmetic teacher had written 10.9 on the blackboard, and had then rubbed out the decimal point to show the effect of multiplying this number by ten.

"Johnson," he asked, "where is the decimal point now?"

"On the eraser, sir!" came the reply.

The teacher was trying to explain the meaning of the word "collision" to a class of small boys.

"If two boys ran into each other in the playground," he said, "what would the result be?"

"A fight, sir," came the answer in chorus.

DAD: "Bert, why are your school reports so bad lately?"

BERT: "Oh, that's the teacher's fault, Dad."

DAD: "What do you mean, it's the teacher's fault? Your marks used to be always very good, and you have the same teacher, haven't you?"

BERT: "Yes, but I don't have the brainiest boy in the class sitting next to me. Teacher moved him!"

Little Sammy Smith was absent from school one Wednesday afternoon. In class the following morning, his teacher said to him, "Sammy Smith, were you playing football again yesterday afternoon?"

"No, sir," said Sammy, "and I've got a jar of minnows to prove it."

TEACHER: "Doreen, I told you to write out this poem twenty times because your handwriting is so bad, and you've only written it out seventeen times."
DOREEN: "My arithmetic's bad as well, teacher."

TEACHER: "Trevor, what do you know about the Dead Sea?"
TREVOR: "I didn't even know it was ill, sir."

TEACHER: "Kevin, why are you late for school?"
KEVIN: "Well, sir, I was dreaming about this football game and it went into overtime, so I had to stay asleep to see the finish!"

Two boys were scrapping in the background when a teacher came by. He pulled them apart and said, "You know the school rules—no fighting allowed."

"But we weren't fighting aloud," they protested. "We were fighting quietly!"

Teacher had assigned his class an essay, "A Game of Baseball." After two minutes Simon Steel handed his paper in and was allowed to go home. His essay read: "Rain stopped play."

TEACHER: "Kevin, you're late for school again. What's the excuse this time?"

KEVIN: "Oh, sir, it was that new sign outside the playground in the street. I would have been here on time, but it says, 'School—Go Slow,' so I had to stop running."

Long after the rest of the school had gone into their class rooms, Alison was still running around in the playground. Her teacher came out and said sharply, "Alison, don't you know the bell has gone?"

"Well, Miss, I didn't take it!"

DAD: "Well, Stephen, did you get a good place in your exams?"

STEPHEN: "Yes, Dad—next to the radiator."

TEACHER: "Jason, which is farther away—England or the moon?"

JASON: "England—you can see the moon, but you can't see England.

ART TEACHER: "Patricia, I told the class to draw a horse and cart, but you've only drawn a horse."
PATRICIA: "Yes, sir—the horse will draw the cart."

ART TEACHER: "Patricia, I told the class to draw a cow eating grass, but you've only drawn a cow."
PATRICIA: "Yes, sir—the cow's eaten all the grass."

TEACHER: "Sarah, what was the first thing James the First did on coming to the throne?"
SARAH: "He sat down, miss."

"The arts and crafts teacher doesn't like what I'm making."
    "Oh? What are you making, then?"
    "Mistakes."

COOKING TEACHER: "Helen, what are the best things to put in a fruitcake?"
HELEN: "Teeth!"

One day, Helen went home and said to her mother, "Mom, I'm not to go to cooking classes anymore." Naturally her mom asked her why.

"Because I burnt something," said Helen.

"And what did you burn?" said Mom.

"The classroom."

TEACHER: "Kevin, why are you late this time?"

KEVIN: "Please, sir, I bruised two fingers knocking in a nail at home."

TEACHER: "I don't see any bandage."

KEVIN: "Oh, they weren't *my* fingers!"

TEACHER: "Gregory, you've put two t's in 'rabbit'—there should be only one."

GREGORY: "Oh. Which t should I have left out, sir?"

"I'm our school champion in the hundred-yard dash."

"Are you really? What do you do it in?"

"Oh, the usual white singlet, shorts, and running shoes!"

"Ha, ha! I bet I could beat you if you give me a yard start."

"Okay, you're on. Where?"

"Up a ladder."

NEW TEACHER: "Doreen, I understand that English grammar is your favorite subject. What tense have I just spoken in?"

DOREEN: "Pre-tense, miss."

TEACHER: "Matthew, what is the climate of New Zealand?"

MATTHEW: "Very cold, sir."

TEACHER: "Wrong."

MATTHEW: "But, sir! When they send us meat it always arrives frozen!"

A hillbilly dragged his protesting son to a new school that had just opened in a nearby township.

On arrival at the school, the hillbilly dad asked the teacher, "What kind of larnin' are ya a-teachifyin'?"

The teacher replied, "Well, all the usual subjects. Reading, writing, arithmetic—"

The earnest dad interrupted him, "What's this here arith . . . arith—what you said?"

"Arithmetic, sir," repeated the teacher. "I shall be giving a full course of geometry, algebra, trigonometry—"

"Triggernometry!" cried the hillbilly. "Dang me! That's just what my boy needs—he's the worsest shot in the family!"

TEACHER: ". . . and as you know, heat causes expansion and cold contraction. Elliot, can you give me an example?"

ELLIOT: "Yes, sir. In summer, when it's hot, the days are longer than in the winter, when it's cold."

TEACHER: "Anyone here quick at picking up music?"

TERENCE AND TONY: "I am, sir!"

TEACHER: "Right, you two. Move that piano!"

TEACHER: "Archie, if you were in a sailboat a mile from the harbor's mouth and a storm blew up, what would you do?"

ARCHIE: "Throw the anchor out, sir."

TEACHER: "And suppose another storm blew up, then what would you do?"

ARCHIE: "Throw out another anchor, sir."

TEACHER: ". . . Er . . . I see. And suppose yet another storm blew up."

ARCHIE: "I'd throw out yet another anchor, sir."

TEACHER: "Just a minute—where are you getting all these anchors from?"

ARCHIE: "The same place as you're getting all the storms from, sir."

A keen young teacher wanted to introduce her class to the glories of classical music, so she arranged an outing to an

afternoon concert. To make the occasion even more memorable, she treated everyone to lemonade, cakes, and ices. Just as the party was getting back into their coach, she said to little Sally, "Have you enjoyed yourself today?"

"Oh, yes!" said Sally. "It was lovely. All except the music, that is."

ALFRED: "Sir, should someone be punished for something they haven't done?"
TEACHER: "No, of course not."
ALFRED: "Good, 'cause I haven't done my homework."

TEACHER: "Harris, when is the best time to gather fruit?"
HARRIS: "When the vicar's dog's tied up, sir!"

A boring teacher was droning on one hot summer's afternoon when he spotted what looked like one of his students reading under the desk.

"Lambert!" he snapped. "What are you doing? Learning something?"

"Oh, no, sir," said Lambert, all innocence. "I'm listening to you, sir."

TEACHER: "Barbara, finish off this proverb: one good turn..."

BARBARA: "One good turn gives you all the blankets!"

TEACHER: "Huntley, what is the imperative of the verb 'to go'?"

HUNTLEY: "Dunno, sir."

TEACHER: "Go, Huntley, Go!"

HUNTLEY: "Thank you very much, sir."

TEACHER: "Nigel, I have your English exercise book here. It is my duty to inform you that b-r-i-x does not spell 'bricks.'"

NIGEL: "Oh? What does it spell then, sir?"

TEACHER: "Michael, if the earth is round, why don't we fall off?"

MICHAEL: "The law of gravity, sir."

TEACHER: "Correct."

VICTOR: "But sir, what happened before the law was passed?"

*Why do cows wear bells?*
   Their horns don't work.

*What language do they speak in Cuba?*
    Cubic.

*Why is a naughty boy like the letter D?*
    Both make ma mad.

*How many legs has a horse?*
    Six: fore-legs in front and two in back.

*What turns without moving?*
    Milk—when it turns sour.

*What can you touch, see, and make but can't hold?*
    A shadow.

*What has six legs, four ears, and a tail?*
    A man on a horse.

*How many feet are there in a field with three hundred sheep, three dogs, two horses, and a farmer?*
    Two, because all the rest are hooves and paws.

*Why do birds fly south in the winter?*
  Because it's too far to walk.

*If a man has ten sons and each son has a sister, how many children has he altogether?*
  Eleven, because the daughter is each son's sister.

*Who is always being let down by his mates?*
  A deep-sea diver.

*What would happen if pigs could fly?*
  Bacon would go up.

*Have you heard the story about the slippery eel?*
  You wouldn't grasp it.

*Have you heard the story about the peacock?*
  It's a beautiful tale [tail]...

*Have you heard the story about the skyscraper?*
  It's a tall story.

The local vicar was paying a visit to the school, visiting each classroom in turn. At one particular class he entered beaming, greeting the teacher and the children, and then said, "Well, what shall I talk to you about?"

At which a small voice at the back growled, "About five minutes!"

TEACHER: "Jane, what comes after G?"
JANE: "Whiz!"
TEACHER: "Let's try again. What comes after U?"
JANE: "The bogeyman!"
TEACHER: "Last chance. What comes after T?"
JANE: "Supper!"

TEACHER: "Miles, what do you call someone who drives an automobile?"
MILES: "Depends how close he misses you, sir."

TEACHER: "Mason, what is the outer part of a tree called?"
MASON: "Don't know, sir."
TEACHER: "Bark, boy, bark!"
MASON: "Woof woof!"

TEACHER: "Where is the River Thames?"
NORMAN: "You're the geography teacher—you tell me!"

TEACHER: "In 1940, what were the Poles doing in Russia?"
IRENE: "Holding up the telegraph wires."

One unfortunate teacher started off a lesson with the following instruction: "I want you all to give me a list of the lower animals, starting with Georgina Clark..."

TEACHER: "Stone, give me three reasons why you know the Earth to be round."
STONE: "Ma says so, Pa says so, and you say so!"

TEACHER: "You seem to be exceedingly ignorant, Williams. Have you read Dickens?"
WILLIAMS: "No, sir."
TEACHER: "Have you read Shakespeare?"
WILLIAMS: "No, sir."
TEACHER: "Well, what *have* you read?"
WILLIAMS: "Er ... er ... I've red hair, sir."

TEACHER: "Marcia, where are elephants found?"
MARCIA: "Dunno, miss. But they're so big I shouldn't think they're often lost, are they?"

SCHOOL INSPECTOR: "Would anyone like to ask me a question?"
IMPERTINENT BOY: "When are you going?"

TEACHER: "Smith, what is moss?"
SMITH: "It's stuff that rolling stones don't gather, sir."

TEACHER: "Gillian, what kinds of birds do we usually find in captivity?"
GILLIAN: "Jailbirds, miss."

TEACHER: "Saunders, can you you tell me what nationality was Napoleon Bonaparte?"
SAUNDERS: "Corsican!"

"How do you spell wrong?"
   "R-o-n-g."
"That's wrong."
"That's what you asked for, wasn't it?"

193

TEACHER: "Georgina, there was the Ice Age, then the Stone Age. What came next?"
GEORGINA: "The saus-age!"

MUSIC TEACHER: "Brian, if f means forte, what does ff mean?"
BRIAN: "Eighty!"

"If a quadruped has four legs and a biped has two legs, what is a zebra?"
   "A stri-ped!"

"Why is it you can never answer any of my questions?"
   "If I could there wouldn't be much point in my coming here!"

"Who spilled that ink on the floor? Come on, own up. . . . Was it you, Faulkner?"
   "I cannot tell a lie, sir. Yes, I done it."
   "Where's your grammar?"
   "In bed with flu."

"Maurice, if you bought thirty jam tarts for twenty cents, what would each one be?"

"Stale..."

A principal about to punish a particularly naughty boy said to him the time-honored words "Bend down, boy—this is going to hurt me more than it will you."

To which the lad replied, "Can I wallop you then, sir?"

"What's your name, boy?"

"Henry."

"Say 'sir.'"

"All right, Sir Henry..."

"Boy, why do you have cotton in your ear? Is it infected?"

"No, sir, but you said yesterday that everything you told me went in one ear and out of the other, so I'm trying to stop it!"

"Kevin, why are you late?"

"I must have overwashed."

HISTORY TEACHER: "Emma, name the Tudor monarchs."
EMMA: "Yes, miss. Henry the Seventh, Henry the Eighth, Edward the Sixth, Mary, er . . . er . . ."
HISTORY TEACHER: "Correct so far. Now who came after Mary?"
EMMA: "Er . . . the little lamb, miss?"

"David, your figures are so bad; that nine looks like a seven."

"It is a seven, sir."

"Then why does it look like a nine?"

"Margaret, you mustn't use 'a' before a plural—you say a horse, not a horses."

"But teacher, the vicar's always saying 'a-men.' . . ."

CHEMISTRY TEACHER: "Robinson, give me the name of a liquid that won't freeze."
ROBINSON: "Hot water, sir?"

TEACHER: "Rosemary, what do we get from Germany?"
ROSEMARY: "Germs?"

COOKING TEACHER: "Gwyneth, how can we prevent food from going bad?"
GWYNETH: "By eating it, miss."

"Kevin, why are you always late?"
    "'Cause you're always ringing the bell before I get here!"

"Raymond, in what battle was Admiral Lord Nelson killed?"
    "His last one, sir."

*Why is a mouse like fresh hay?*
    Because the cattle [cat'll] eat it.

*Who is the smallest sailor in the world?*
    The one who slept on his watch.

*Why do people laugh up their sleeves?*
    Because that's where their funnybone is.

*Which is bigger—Mrs. Bigger or Baby Bigger?*
  Baby Bigger, because he's a little Bigger.

*Why did the lobster blush?*
  'Cause he saw the salad dressing.

*What did Rome-o?*
  For what Juli-et.

*What is the noisiest of all games?*
  Tennis, because you can't play it without raising a racket.

*What is it you can put in your right hand but not in your left?*
  Your left elbow.

At an examination, the teacher thought that he spotted one of the boys peeping at another boy's paper. He went to the boy's desk and said, "Hogan, I hope I didn't see you looking at this boy's paper."

To which Hogan replied, "I hope so too, sir!"

TEACHER: "Marion, why weren't you in school yesterday?"

MARION: "I had a bad tooth, miss."

TEACHER: "Oh, I'm sorry to hear that. Is it better now?"

MARION: "Dunno, miss. I left it with the dentist."

HISTORY TEACHER: "Skinner, when did motor cars first appear on the streets?"

SKINNER: "In the reign of King John, sir."

HISTORY TEACHER: "In the reign of King John? How do you make that out?"

SKINNER: "Well, sir, you told us that King John was always grinding the people down with taxis."

Judy was spotted by her teacher with a large bulge in her cheek.

"Judith!" said the teacher sternly. "What have you got in your mouth? Bring it here!"

"I wish I could, teacher," said poor Judith. "It's a gumboil."

One small boy on his first day in school was being interviewed by the school secretary.

"Father's name?" asked the secretary, filling in a big official form.

"Same as mine," answered the child, in some bewilderment.

"No, no, no," said the secretary. "I mean his Christian name."

"Oh, I dunno, miss," said the child.

"Well, what does your mother call him?"

"She doesn't call him anything—she likes him!"

TEACHER: "If eggs were twenty cents a dozen, how many would you get for five cents?"

PUPIL: "None."

TEACHER: "None?"

PUPIL: If I had five cents I'd get a bar of toffee crunch."

TEACHER: "Why weren't you at school yesterday?"

SEAN: "I was sick."

TEACHER: "Sick of what?"

SEAN: "Sick of school!"

TEACHER: "Kevin, why are you late yet again?"

KEVIN: "Oh, sir, I stopped two boys fighting."

TEACHER: "How did you manage that?"

KEVIN: "I licked both of 'em!"

TEACHER: "Rosemary, I wish you'd pay a little attention."
ROSEMARY: "I'm paying as little as I can, miss!"

# Rhymes without Reason

She stood on the bridge at midnight,
Her lips were all aquiver;
She gave a cough, her leg fell off
And floated down the river!

There was a young lady from Jarrow
Whose mouth was exceedingly narrow;
She ate with a spoon
By the light of the moon,
But all she could eat was a marrow!

A charming young singer named Hannah,
Got caught in a flood in Savannah;
As she floated away,

Her sister—they say;
Accompanied her on the piannah!

There was a young man from Dumbarton,
Who thought he could run like a Spartan.
On the thirty-ninth lap
His braces went snap,
And his face went a red Scottish tartan.

A flea and a fly in a flue,
Were trapped, so they thought, "What to do?"
"Let us fly," said the flea,
"Let us flee," said the fly,
So they flew through a flaw in the flue!

An earnest young fisher named Fisher
Once fished from the edge of a fissure.
A fish with a grin
Pulled the fisherman in—
Now they're fishing the fissure for Fisher!

There was a young lady from Riga,
Who rode with a smile on a tiger.
They returned from the ride

With the lady inside,
And the smile on the face of the tiger.

An old lady who came from Kilbride,
Ate so many apples—she died!
The apples fermented
Inside the lamented—
Making cider inside 'er inside!

There was a young man from Leeds,
Who swallowed a packet of seeds;
Within just one hour
His nose was a flower
And his head was a riot of weeds!

There was a young man from Bengal,
Who was asked to a fancy-dress ball.
He said he would risk it
And went as a biscuit,
But a dog ate him up in the hall!

There once was a chief of the Sioux,
Who into a gun-barrel blioux
To see if 'twas loaded;

The rifle exploded—
As he should have known it would dioux!

There was a young man from Quebec
Who wrapped both his legs 'round his neck!
But then he forgot
How to undo the knot,
And now he's an absolute wreck!

There once was a writer named Wright,
Who instructed his son to write right;
He said, "Son, write Wright right.
It is not right to write
Wright as 'rite'—try to write Wright aright!"

There was an old man from Whitehaven,
Whose whiskers had never been shaven;
He said, "It is best,
For they make a nice nest,
In which I can keep my pet raven!"

There once was a fat boy called Kidd,
Who ate twenty mince pies for a quid.
When asked "Are you faint?"

He replied, "No, I ain't,
But I don't feel as well as I did!"

I eat peas with honey,
I've done it all my life.
They do taste kind of funny—
But it keeps them on the knife!

Sweet little Emily Rose,
Was tired and sought some repose.
But her sister named Clare
Put a tack on her chair,
And sweet little Emily Rose!

There was an old man from Carlisle,
Who sat down one day on a stile.
The paint it was wet,
So he's sitting there yet;
But he hopes to get off with a file!

There was an old man from Penzance,
Who always wore sheet-iron pants;

He said, "Some years back,
I sat on a tack,
And I'll never again take a chance!"

# Amaze Your Friends

## and infuriate your enemies

An easy trick at a party is to say that you will go out of the room, and in your absence you want any lady present and any gentleman present to place a coin on the table—and you will be able to tell which coin belongs to the man and which to the woman! The secret is that when you come back into the room you must pick up each of the coins; one will feel warmer than the other—this is the man's, since the coin will have been warmed by his body. The woman's coin, on the other hand, will have been in her handbag and so will be quite cold.

You can make a matchbox appear to rise of its own accord by shutting it over a fold of skin of your knuckle. Try it and see!

Invite a friend to breathe on your magic mirror to see what it will tell him. As he breathes on the mirror, sure enough

a ghostly message appears! The secret of this is simplicity itself: before your friend enters the room simply mark the mirror with whatever message you wish him to read (i.e. "You are a silly fool!") *with your finger*. Believe it or not, this will not show up until he breathes on it!

Put ten matches on the table and invite a friend to make a monkey from them. When he fails, simply arrange the matches into the word "APE," using two matches for the top of the letter P. Similarly, seven matches can be used to make a hotel. It may seem impossible, until you use the seven matches to spell out the word "INN"—which is a kind of hotel, isn't it?

Challenge a friend to pick up a brush without touching it; your solution is to produce a second brush which you push firmly down onto the bristles of the first!

Make a fist; place a playing card on the back of your hand and a coin on the card. Then announce that you will remove the card without touching the coin. The solution? You simply flick the card with your left hand. If you get the angle right (it needs a slightly downward flick) the card will go sailing away but the coin will remain.

PATSY: "I bet I can make you say 'black.'"

MIKE: "Go on, then."

PATSY: "What are colors of the flag?"

MIKE: "Red, white, and blue."

PATSY: "There you are. I told you I could make you say 'blue.'"

MIKE: "No—you said you could make me say 'black.'"

PATSY: "And you've just said it, haven't you?"

Tell a friend that you have 11 fingers. When he scoffs at this claim, count from 1 to 10 on your fingers; then count backward, saying, "10, 9, 8, 7, 6—and 5 fingers on the other hand makes 11!"

A mystifying illusion is to tell your friends that you can push a chalk cross through a solid table. You take a piece of chalk, draw a small cross on a table or chair, then put one hand under the table while pushing hard on the cross with the other. After a few seconds, the cross on the top is gone and—lo and behold!—there is a little chalk cross on the palm of your other hand.

The secret is very simple. Before starting you draw a small chalk cross on the nail of your second finger. Although the palm of your hand can be examined closely and even washed, no one ever thinks of looking at your nails. So while this hand is under the table or chair, you just close

your fist, press hard and the chalk cross will be transferred to the ball of your thumb. The hand on top of course simply rubs the chalk cross out.

The following story is a good one to tell at parties:

"I am going to tell you a story about three little ducks. Will you help me? Thank you. Now these three little ducks were called—(*here you hold up one finger*) Quack, Quack-Quack (*hold up two fingers*), and Quack-Quack-Quack (*hold up three fingers*). Shall we try that again? Three little ducks called Quack (*one finger*), Quack-Quack (*two fingers*), and Quack-Quack-Quack (*three fingers*).

"Now, one day these three little ducks decided to go into the country to collect some mushrooms, to make a lovely mushroom soup. So out they went and collected a huge basketful of mushrooms; they went home and made their lovely mushroom soup. But in the middle of the night— (*hold up one finger*)—fell ill! So (*two fingers*) . . . said to (*three fingers*) . . . "you'd better go and get the doctor."

"Well, the doctor came and examined (*one finger*), and said, "Oh, he's just got a touch of indigestion, he'll be all right in the morning. Just give him these pills. And so, greatly relieved, (*two fingers*) . . . and (*three fingers*) . . . gave (*one finger*) the pills. But by the time morning came, (*one finger*) had died! (*Aaaaah!*) At which (*two fingers*) . . . said to (*three fingers*) . . . "I think that doctor must have been a bit of a (*one finger*)! Thank you."

Say to a friend who is wearing a coat or a jacket, "I bet you can't button your coat up." When he has fastened the buttons, which he will do immediately to prove you wrong, you then say, "There, I told you you couldn't button it *up*"—because everyone buttons from the top *down*.

How to tie a knot in a piece of string without letting go of the ends: fold your arms, pick up the string with an end in each hand, then unfold your arms. Presto—a knot is made!

Try this one on a friend, and you can be sure you'll catch him or her out.

"What does T O spell?"

"To."

"And what does T O O spell?"

"Too."

"What does T W O spell?"

"Two."

"And what is the second day of the week?"

"Tuesday."

"No—Monday is the second day of the week!"

Another party gag: Put a glass of water under a hat and announce that you will drink the water without touching

the hat! Amid sounds of disbelief, you crouch down behind the hat—hiding your face from view and make slurping sounds as though drinking. Then you stand up and say, "There you are!" Someone is bound to lift the hat to see whether the water is gone from the glass. As soon as this happens you calmly pick up the glass and drink *without touching the hat*—as promised!

You can continue with this gag: Place the empty glass on the table upside down. Then place on the table three matches and invite one of the parties to place one of the matches on top of the glass, using only the other two matches. After some difficulty, he will do this. "But," you will say, "I told you to put the match on the top of the glass—and you've put it on the bottom!"

You can then show everyone a small colored disc of cardboard and three egg cups. You say that you will turn your back—or even go out of the room—while the disc is placed under one of the egg cups. When you return you will be able to tell which one the disc is under. The secret is that beforehand you have stuck a hair onto the disc with some gum; the hair, which will be undetectable to anyone not in on the secret, will stick out from underneath the egg cup (provided you don't make the disc too small) enabling you to work the trick instantly. Take a little time over it, though—you don't want to make it look too easy!

This one is simply astounding to anyone not in the know: to begin you show a skeleton cut out of cardboard and colored white, and about twelve inches in height—it helps if the limbs can be jointed with staples. This can be handled and examined by your audience. You then place the skeleton upright between the legs of a table or chair at one end of the room—and the skeleton not only stands unaided but dances to your command! You can then pick up the skeleton, again hand it around for examination, and repeat the trick as often as required.

The secret is this: before the start of your party, you push a pin into the back of each of the two legs of the table or chair under which your skeleton is to dance. These pins should be placed at about the height of the skeleton's shoulders. You then attach a piece of black cotton to one of the pins, and take it across to the other pin. The cotton is not attached to the second pin—it merely rests on it, and continues to the nearest chair. In this chair is sitting your accomplice . . . now you can see how the skeleton dances. As you turn to place the skeleton beneath the table or chair, your accomplice picks up the other end of the cotton and pulls it taut. You place the arms of the skeleton behind the cotton and step back. On the command, "Skeleton, dance!" your accomplice merely has to jerk the cotton very gently—and your skeleton does just that!

You can be sure that if the lights are lowered and your skeleton is carefully painted, the cotton will not be seen.

214

The following coin trick was demonstrated to the author by his father over a period of five or six years without the secret displaying itself, so you can try it with confidence! The effect is this:

You pick up a coin and show it for examination. You then place your elbow on a table with your arm bent and slap the coin on to your forearm, rubbing it up and down between your wrist and elbow with four fingers of the other hand. You take away one finger, still rubbing, then another, then another, and finally take away the remaining finger to show that the coin has disappeared! The coin (which can be marked to show there is no substitution) can then be produced from your ear, or your pocket, or wherever you choose.

The secret is the old illusionist technique of misdirection. When you first start to rub the coin on your arm, you "accidentally" drop it; you pick it up and again start to rub—and again you "accidentally" drop it. The third time you pick it up with the *other hand*, i.e., the hand that does not do the rubbing. Swiftly, however, you slap the empty hand against your arm and start to rub—I can guarantee that this will not be spotted. I have even tried it on grown-ups and fooled them! With the coin in your other hand, you can then produce it from wherever you like.

Another party trick: You announce to company that you will divine any object in the room that they care to choose.

You pick one person as spokesman and leave the room. When you return the spokesman says, "Is it the television set? Is it the clock on the mantelpiece? Is it the mirror on the wall?—and so on, until he mentions the article chosen, which you instantly identify.

The secret is that the spokesman is an accomplice. As you leave the room you quite naturally put your hand on the door to shut it. The number of fingers displayed as you do this will indicate to him or her when to indicate the chosen article. In other words, if you show three fingers, then the article chosen by the company will be the third one named by the spokesman. Very simple, but remarkably effective.

This card trick will make your friends' eyes pop out with amazement. The effect is this: You ask one of your friends to think of a pack of cards. You then ask him to tell you his preference as to color—red or black. Now ask him which suit he would prefer—if he chooses black he must decide between clubs or spades. Then you ask whether he would like a picture card or a number card. If he chooses a picture card, you continue as follows.

"We'll divide the picture cards into two pairs—jack and queen, and king and ace. Which do you choose? The jack and queen? Right—now let's take them one at a time. Do you choose the jack *or* the queen? The jack—very well, that leaves the queen. And you earlier chose clubs, didn't you? So you have now selected the queen of clubs. Would

you look in the left-hand pocket of your jacket, please?"

And sure enough, the queen of clubs will be found in the left-hand pocket of your friend's jacket—a card chosen at random by himself!

How to do it? The secret is that the card to be discovered is planted by you in advance. It can be any card—say, the two of hearts—which you will slip into your friend's jacket pocket or put in the leaves of a book in a cupboard or seal in an envelope or anywhere you want. Now, the way you ask the questions is all-important, for although you appear to offer a choice, in fact you lead the questioning *in the required direction all the time.* Let's try it with the two of hearts:

"Which color do you choose—red or black?"

"Black."

"Very well, that leaves red. Hearts or diamonds?"

"Hearts."

"Hearts. Now, will you have number cards or picture cards?"

"Picture cards."

"That leaves number cards. Now, I'll divide them up into two: two to five, or six to ten. Which half will you have?"

"Two to five."

"And now I'll divide those into two pairs: two and three, four and five. Which do you choose?"

"Four and five."

"That leaves two and three. Which of those cards will you choose?"

"Two."

"The two of hearts—and here it is!"

217

Do you see now how the questioning leads on to the card? If your friend makes the correct choice for the card you have preselected, you just carry on. If, however, he makes the wrong choice, you just say, "Very well, that leaves—" and you carry on with the right choice.

This trick is an absolute baffler, but don't do it more than once or the secret will become apparent!

Try this one on your mom or dad. Say, "I bet I can get you to clasp your hands together so that you won't be able to leave the room without undoing them." When this challenge is accepted, you just get your victim to clasp his or her hands together round a piano leg or the leg of the telly stand or any heavy piece of furniture. Sure enough, they won't be able to leave the room without unclasping their hands!

"Here, Norman, you'd better keep your eyes open today."
"Why?"
"If you don't you'll keep banging into things."

Here's a trick that's bound to catch someone. Ask them to write down on a piece of paper eleven thousand, eleven hundred and eleven. The correct answer is 12111—but you'll nearly always be given the wrong one!

Ask a pal if he can write "fifty miles under the sea" in four words. When he admits defeat, show him the solution: Easy when you know how, eh?

$$\frac{the\ sea}{fifty\ miles}$$

If a man is locked in a prison cell with only a wooden chair, how can he get out?

First of all he rubs his hands together till they're sore; then he takes the saw and saws the chair in half. Two halves make a whole, so he crawls through the hole and then shouts till he is hoarse. Then all he has to do is to jump on the horse and gallop away!

Here's a great party trick: Put three candies on the table and cover them with three hats. Lift the first hat, pick up the candy, and eat it; do the same with the second and the third. Now for the magic! You say to the assembled company, "And now, ladies and gentlemen, which hat would you like to be covering the three sweets?" And when someone unsuspectingly points to one of the hats, you simply pick it up and put it on your head!

Here's a neat trick: Take three handkerchiefs, one colored and the other two white. Tie them together with the colored one at the end, and then ask a friend whether he can put the colored handkerchief *between* the white ones without untying any knots. When he is unable to do so, you demonstrate how it is done, by simply tying the free ends of the handkerchiefs together. You now have a circle of hankies, and the colored one is between the white ones!

Here's a game that you can always win. Put sixteen matches on the table and challenge a friend to remove either one or two matches; you will then also remove one or two. Then it is his turn again, then yours and so on. The point of the game is that the loser is the one who has to take the last match. So how do you always win?

First, your challenger must always *start first*; second, if he takes one match, you must take *two* and if he takes two matches you must take *one*. In this way he will always be the one to take the last match and so lose the game!

Cut a small hole in a piece of paper and challenge a friend to push his finger through the center of the paper. When he fails to do so, simply roll the paper up into a cylinder and push your finger down the center of the roll!

How to cut a square in a piece of paper with one snip of the scissors. Fold the paper in two and then in two again. Now all you have to do is to cut straight across the folded corner. Unfold the paper and there is a perfect square!

Ask a friend to take a coin out of his pocket and hold it tightly in his hand: by concentrating hard with your hand on his or her head you will be able to tell the date. After screwing your eyes up, with every appearance of racking your brains you eventually say, "Yes . . . I have it, I think . . . the date is—" And then you give today's date!

Take a piece of paper and a pencil and announce to a friend, "I can write with my left ear!" When he challenges you to do so, simply take up the pencil and write "with my left ear"!

A similar trick is to announce that you can sing underwater. When challenged to prove this unlikely boast, you merely sing the words "under water" to a popular tune! ("Daisy, Daisy" is a good one for this.)

This is bound to catch somebody: ask which of the following two statements is correct—the yolk of an egg *are* white or the yolk of an egg *is* white? Almost certainly you will be told that "the yolk of an egg *is* white" is correct; whereupon you point out that the yolk of an egg is yellow!

Another challenge: ask a friend to add 2 to 91 and make it less? It sounds impossible, until you write it this way:

$$\frac{91}{2} \quad (9\frac{1}{2})$$

Everyone knows that there are twenty-six letters in the alphabet, but you can prove that there are only eleven letters in the alphabet. And how do you do this? Quite simply—by counting out the letters as you write "t-h-e a-l-p-h-a-b-e-t"!

Mystify a pal by saying that you are about to show him or her something which has never been seen before by human eyes and will never be seen again. You then open a peanut shell and swallow the peanut!

Tie a pencil to one end of a piece of string and hold it up by the other end. Now you state that you will cut through the string but the pencil will not fall to the floor. To perform this amazing feat you simply tie a loop in the string, and then cut through the loop!

Ask a pal whether he can take half away from something and leave more? When he fails to think of anything—as you can be sure he will—you write down the word: HALFPENNY. Then all you have to do is to scratch through HALF with your pencil, leaving PENNY—which is more than you started with!

If you put seven matches on the table, how can you take away one and leave none? By simply arranging the six remaining matches into the word NIL!

Here's a neat trick: put three matchboxes on the table and explain that only one of them has matches in it. Pick up each box in turn and shake it—only one will rattle. You then change the three boxes around rapidly and challenge the company present to guess which is the box with the matches in. No one will ever get it right. And why is this? Because none of the boxes has any matches in it! How do you get one to rattle, then? You have *another* box with

some matches in it attached to your arm with a rubber band (you must keep your jacket on for this trick of course), so that when you shake a box with that hand your audience will hear a rattle. To demonstrate the two "empty" boxes you just shake them with the other hand.

You can bet your bottom dollar you can catch a pal with this gag. Say to him, "There's only one way of making money." And when he says, "What's that?" as he certainly will, your swift reply is "I thought *you* wouldn't know it!"

You can be sure of getting a laugh at your party with this trick. Take an ordinary object, such as a box or a newspaper, and announce to a guest that you will place it in full view of everyone else, but that you will hypnotize him so that he will not be able to see it.

Then, having made a few suitable passes in front of his face, you simply place the object on his head. In that position, of course, everyone will be able to see it but the person underneath. Make sure that there are no mirrors around, though, or the tables may be turned on you!

# Lucky Dip (2)

TOMMY: "I had a rotten vacation this year!"
FRED: "Why's that?"
TOMMY: "The weather was lousy. We went to the zoo, but all we saw was the keeper building an ark."

JACK: "Mom just got a letter from my brother in Australia."
MARK: "How's he doing?"
JACK: "As big a flop as ever. He tried to go surf riding, but he couldn't get the horse into the water."

## *Foreign Phrases*

*Sic transit gloria mundi*—My big sister was ill on the bus
going back to school after the
weekend.

*Pas de deux*—Father of twins.
*Coq au vin*—A chicken on a truck.

The cheapest man in the world went to the dentist with a toothache.

"I'm afraid they'll all have to come out," said the dentist gravely.

"How much will that cost?" asked the man.

"Twenty dollars."

"Here's five dollars. Just loosen them a bit."

TEACHER: "Today we are going to study *Macbeth* by Shakespeare."

BOASTFUL PUPIL: "My dad had dinner with Shakespeare last night."

TEACHER: "But he's been dead for over three hundred years!"

PUPIL: "Oh, really? Dad said he was a bit quiet."

MIKE: "My brother's a puppeteer."

JOHN: "How did he get a job like that?"

MIKE: "Oh, he pulled a few strings."

SADIE: "I think my brother must be mad."

SARAH: "What makes you say that?"

SADIE: "He thinks he's a dog."
SARAH: "How long has this been going on?"
SADIE: "Ever since he was a puppy."

A motorist was driving along the motorway when, to his amazement, he was overtaken by a cyclist.

He increased his speed to eighty miles per hour, but once again the cyclist passed him, pedaling furiously. Eventually, the driver could stand it no longer and stopped.

"Thank heavens you've stopped," said the cyclist. "I had my suspenders caught in your back bumper."

TRAMP: "'Scuse me sir. Have you got a dollar for a meal?"
CHEAP MAN: "No."
TRAMP: "Well, have you got fifty cents for a bowl of soup?"
CHEAP MAN: "No."
TRAMP: "Well, you'd better take my jacket—you're worse off than I am."

ALFIE: "That's a fierce-looking Alsatian you've got there. Bet he's a good watchdog."
TOM: "All he watches is television."

COLIN: "My dad's a big-game hunter in Scotland. He shoots lions."

JERRY: "But there aren't any lions in Scotland."
COLIN: "Not now there aren't. He shot 'em all."

FOREIGN TOURIST (to man carrying violin case): "Excuse me. How do I get to the Carnegie Hall?"
VIOLINIST: "Practice."

Another violinist was convinced he could use his art in music to tame wild animals. So, violin in hand, he traveled to the heart of the African jungle to prove it.

He had no sooner begun to play than the jungle clearing was filled with animals of all kinds gathering to hear him play. Birds, lions, hippos, elephants—all stood around, entranced by his beautiful music.

Just then a crocodile crept out of the nearby river and into the clearing, and—snap!—gobbled up the violinist.

The other animals were extremely irate.

"What on earth did you do that for?" they demanded. "We were enjoying that."

"Eh?" said the crocodile, cupping its hand to its ear.

WANTED FOR THEFT: Man with one eye called Jones.

The unluckiest man in the world: the deep-sea diver coming up who met his ship going down.

TEACHER: "Late again. What's the excuse this time?"

PUPIL: "Sorry, teacher. There was a notice on the bus saying "Dogs must be carried," and I couldn't find one anywhere."

A distraught patient called his doctor at two o'clock in the morning.

"I'm very sorry to disturb you at this time of the morning, doctor," he apologized.

"Oh, that's all right," relied the doctor. "I had to get up anyway to answer the phone."

FIRST PASSENGER (at a bus stop): "Do you know how long the next bus will be?"

SECOND PASSENGER: "About twenty-five feet."

BOY: "A bottle of lemonade, please."

CAFÉ OWNER: "How would you like to get one free?"

BOY: "How?"

CAFÉ OWNER: "We're giving one away with every fifty-cent bag of potato chips."

INSURANCE MAN (to prospective client): "What do you keep in the wall safe?"

CLIENT: "The wall."

INSURANCE MAN: "And suppose you have a fire."

CLIENT: "We'll put that in there, too."

PETE: "I haven't slept a wink for the past two nights."

JIMMY: "Why's that?"

PETE: "Granny broke her leg. The doctor put it in plaster and told her she shouldn't walk upstairs. You should hear the noise when she climbs up the drainpipe."